SECOND EDITION THE BEATLES

A REFERENCE & VALUE GUIDE

By Barbara Crawford, Hollis Lamon, and Michael Stern

COLLECTOR BOOKS

A Division of Schroeder Publishing Co., Inc.

The current values of this book should be used only as a guide. They are not intended to set prices, which vary from one section of the country to another. Auction prices as well as dealer prices vary greatly and are affected by condition as well as demand. Neither the Authors nor the Publisher assumes responsibility for any losses that might be incurred as a result of consulting this guide.

Searching for a Publisher?

We are always looking for knowledgeable people considered to be experts within their fields. If you feel that there is a real need for a book on your collectible subject and have a large comprehensive collection, contact Collector Books.

On the cover:
Beatles Purse, Yellow Submarine Candle, Ringo Starr Drum, Beatles Dress from Holland, Set of Beatles Yellow Submarine, Banks by Pride Creations

Cover Design: Beth Summers
Book Design: Joyce Cherry
Printed in the U.S.A. by Image Graphics Inc., Paducah KY

Additional copies of this book may be ordered from:

Collector Books
P.O. Box 3009
Paducah, Kentucky 42002-3009

@ $19.95. Add $2.00 for postage and handling.

Contents

ACKNOWLEDGMENTS

Thanks to Troy McNeilly of Studio 120 for his assistance in photographing the book.

To Barbara Crawford whose photography makes the pictures come to life.

To Joe Hilton who sold us some of the exciting Yellow Submarine merchandise, and whose enthusiasm was invaluable.

To the Beatles for creating such incredible music.

INTRODUCTION

The Beatles influenced and changed a whole generation. They created rock 'n' roll and established rock music as an art form. The Beatles left a mark on the millions of kids who saw and heard them. The Beatles and their music are synonymous with the vibrant times of the 1960s. They did more to influence and impact the youth of the 1960s than did anyone else. The Beatles were trend setters from fashion to hairstyles.

I grew up in this era and remember vividly watching their live appearance on the "Ed Sullivan Show" and taping it on my reel to reel. I experienced their music, and my own life seemed to mirror their changing music as I grew from adolescence to adulthood. From "Meet the Beatles to Sgt. Peppers to the White Album," I was there with them.

This book is not a history of the Beatles. It is an identification and value guide to the artifacts of the 1960s that were created because of them. These items of memorabilia encompassed almost every type of object. If it could be sold, some company created the product with the Beatles' image somewhere on it. If you were one who grew up to the Beatles' music, you will be able to relate to each piece of memorabilia, but I assure you, you will remember only a handful of these items.

The field of rock 'n' roll collecting has come of age and the Beatles, as they did with their music, are leading the way. Today with Hard Rock Cafes being built in most major cities and Beatlefests being held all over the world, there is a refocusing on the Beatles and the collectibles that were made to promote them. All major auction houses, including Christies and Sotheby's, now have rock 'n' roll auctions. In fact, John Lennon's Rolls Royce sold for $2,292,600 at Sotheby's in New York, which put its price in the top ten car prices in the world.

This book will not deal with records or with fan magazines. To me, both of these areas are collecting fields unto themselves. This book deals instead in licensed products that could be bought in stores worldwide during the times that they were produced.

The memorabilia in this book was brought to market in three different time frames; each has its own section in the book. The largest concentration of Beatles memorabilia was created and produced in 1964 and 1965 when the Beatles were in their heyday. Then in 1968, with the release of the movie, Yellow Submarine, stores were stocked with a whole new product line, just in time for Christmas. The third wave of merchandise was when Apple Productions was formed and consisted of promotional pieces

The book also features cels (Yellow Submarine movie celluloids) which is a field of increasing popularity and one in which prices are escalating rapidly.

The collecting of Beatle memorabilia is the collecting of an art form and the appreciation of the prices of this art form parallels the increase in the values of all forms of art work. It could be said that collecting is like buying quality stocks and bonds, an excellent investment that annually increases in value. The added value is that whereas stocks and bonds are tucked away in a safe or vault, your Beatle collectibles can be displayed and enjoyed on a daily basis.

All of the photographs in this book are taken from the collection of Barbara Crawford. Barbara has been a Beatles fanatic for many years and can now boast of one of the premier collections in the world. Her devotion and dedication to achieving this goal have made this book a reality.

Our hope is that this book will help the novice collectors in broadening their scope so that when acquiring a piece of Beatles memorabilia, it can be dated and its price put into perspective.

— Michael Stern

PRICING INFORMATION

This value guide for Beatles collectibles is to be used as a point of reference before buying or selling an item. Any value guide tends to be subjective in nature, and we've used the sources available to us to arrive at what we think are accurate price points in today's marketplace. The Beatles collectible market can change dramatically in a very short span of time.

We have determined the values for each item based on a number of factors and sources:

1. What we have paid for each item.
2. Auction catalogs.
3. Mail auction price realized lists.
4. Toy and doll show prices.
5. Antique trader ads.

We feel the values suggested are excellent estimates of what each item is actually worth. The basic law of economics — supply and demand — can shoot holes through any value guide. "The worth of a collectible is what someone will pay for it," is an adage which is still prevalent for today's collectors.

The following descriptions relate to the condition of the item and how they are priced accordingly.

Good Condition

An item in good condition is in working order, has been used, shows general wear and tear. The item must look fairly clean with little or no rust.

Excellent, Mint Condition

Excellent means the item is clean and looks as if it has never been used. It is complete and all functions are operative. Mint applies to mint in the box (MIB) and means the item is in its original package. In many cases, the box is worth more than the item itself.

Each item has been priced as it appears in the picture (with box, with tag, with label.)

CHAPTER ONE

Early Beatles Memorabilia

This chapter is the largest in the book. It deals with merchandise produced in the early years of the Beatles and their rise to success. Most of the items pictured in this chapter were manufactured in 1964 and 1965.

Brian Epstein, the manager of the Beatles, realized that he could generate substantial profits by selling thousands of different items bearing the Beatles' pictures. He knew the Beatles were a marketable commodity and formed the North End Music Stores to license and approve all Beatles merchandise. They wanted quality products, so their seal of approval was the words "NEMS" which stood for North End Music Stores and was put on licensed products. If the items were produced in the United States, they were marked SELTAEB which is "Beatles" spelled backwards.

For a group that stayed together only seven years, there was an incredible amount of merchandise produced. There was an endless supply and variety from many different countries.

Beware — counterfeits do exist and many have used the "NEMS" marking. Many of the counterfeits are items easily made, such as buttons, playing cards, and soap bubbles. When an item's validity is contingent on just a label, caution is advised.

The key to the pricing of any item is condition, condition, condition!

Plate 1. *Airbed* is a very rare piece manufactured only in England by the Li-Lo Company. It is made of vinyl and can be inflated. Good, $1,000.00; Excellent/Mint, $1,200.00.

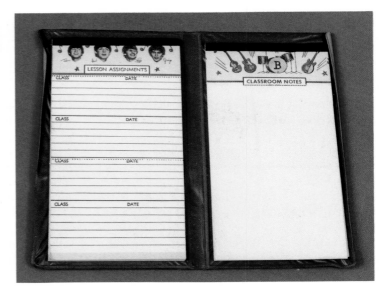

Plate 2. *Assignment Book* was manufactured by Select-O-Pak. It is vinyl and has two note pads included — Lesson Assignments and Classroom Notes. Good, $200.00; Excellent/Mint, $250.00.

Plate 3. *Apron* is a NEMS ENT, Ltd. product. It is made of a paper-like fiber. Good, $400.00; Excellent/Mint, $450.00.

Plate 4. *Ashtray* is made of china. Good, $250.00; Excellent/Mint, $300.00.

Plate 5. *AirFlite Carrying Case* is made of vinyl and is a very desirable collectible. Good, $900.00; Excellent/Mint, $1,100.00.

Plate 6. *AirFlite Carrying Case* came in three colors. This is the red version. Good, $900.00; Excellent/Mint, $1,100.00.

Plate 7. *AirFlite Carrying Case* came in three colors. Black is the rarest variation. Good, $1,200.00; Excellent/Mint, $1,500.00.

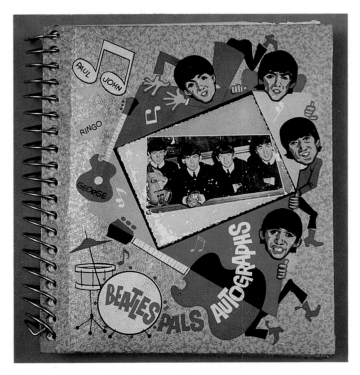

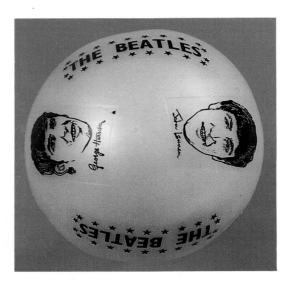

Plate 9. *Ball* is white rubber and is inflatable. It is 8" in diameter. Good, $700.00; Excellent/Mint, $750.00.

Plate 8. *Autograph Book* contains pages for collecting autographs. Very few are known to exist. Good, $600.00; Excellent/Mint, $700.00.

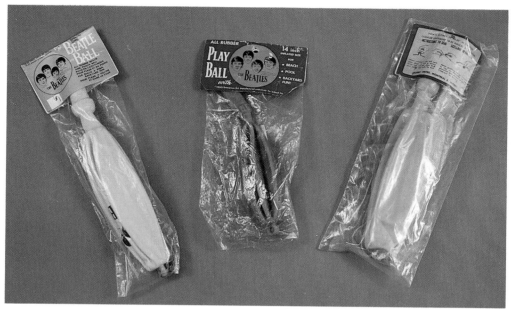

Plate 10. *Balls* of which there are only three known to exist in their original packaging. When inflated, they are 14" in diameter. They were made by the Seltaeb Company and are made of all rubber. Good, $800.00; Excellent/Mint, $900.00.

Plate 11. *Ball* is 9" in diameter and is inflatable. Good, $800.00; Excellent/Mint, $900.00.

Plate 12. *Balloons* were made by the United States Industries of Southington, Connecticut. These items can be found in a variety of colors. The group shot is pictured on each balloon. Good, $50.00; Excellent/Mint, $60.00.

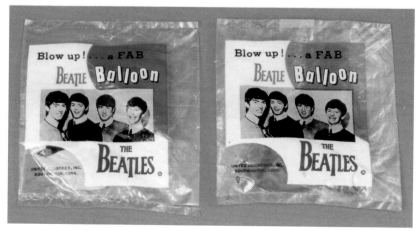

Plate 13. *Bamboo Plates* were produced by the Bamboo Tray Specialist Company. The scene pictured is from *A Hard Day's Night.* Sizes pictured left to right are 11" and 6" in diameter. Good, $120.00; Excellent/Mint, $145.00.

Plate 14. *Bamboo Plate* is the third size and largest. It is 12" in diameter. Good, $120.00; Excellent/Mint, $145.00.

Plate 15. *Brief Cover was* made by Select-O-Pak and came in a variety of colors. Good, $400.00; Excellent/Mint, $450.00.

Plate 16. *Brief Case* was made by Select-O-Pak. This was used inside a notebook. Good, $1,200.00; Excellent/Mint, $1,500.00.

Plate 17. *Binder* was developed to hold the *Beatle Monthly* Magazines. Good, $450.00; Excellent/Mint, $500.00.

Plate 18. *Belts* are made of vinyl and can be found in a variety of colors. Good, $80.00; Excellent/Mint, $90.00.

Plate 19. *Belt Buckle* utilizes a black and white picture of the group surrounded by heavy metal. Good, $100.00; Excellent/Mint, $125.00.

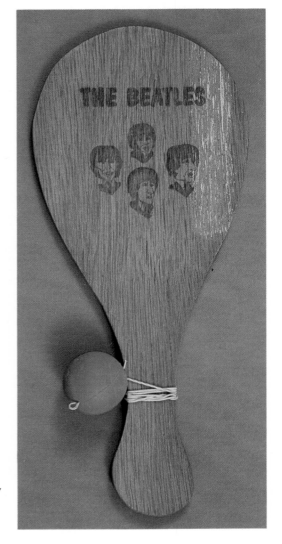

Plate 20. *Bolo Bouncer* is a very unusual item. Good, $100.00; Excellent/Mint, $150.00.

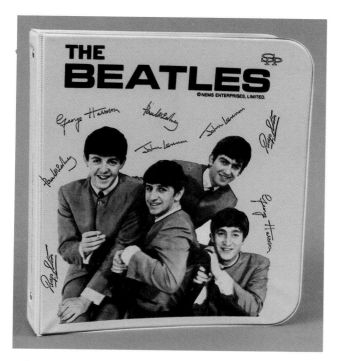

Plate 22. *Binder* in the rare purple color variation. Good, $150.00; Excellent/Mint, $175.00.

Plate 21. *Binder* was produced by New York Loose-leaf Corporation. This is the three-ring variation. They were produced in various colors. Good, $100.00; Excellent/Mint, $125.00.

Plate 23. *Binder* in the turquoise variation. Good, $225.00; Excellent/Mint, $250.00.

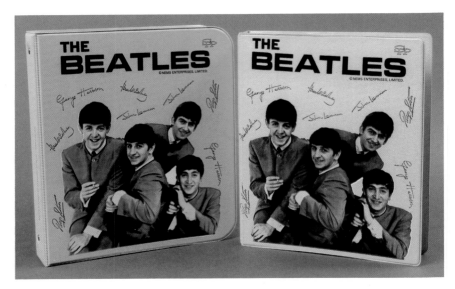

Plate 24. *Binders* were produced in many sizes and hold variations. This is a three-ring and two-ring in the same color. Good, $125.00; Excellent/Mint, $150.00.

Plate 25. *Birth Certificates* are contained in cartoon-like booklets. Good, $75.00. Excellent/Mint, $100.00.

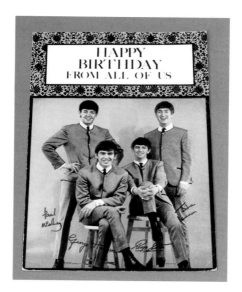

Plate 26. *Birthday Card* was printed by American Greetings. Good, $35.00; Excellent/Mint, $40.00.

Plate 27. *Blanket* was produced by the Witney Company. It is 62" wide and 80" long. It is made of wool and fiber. Good, $400.00; Excellent/Mint, $450.00.

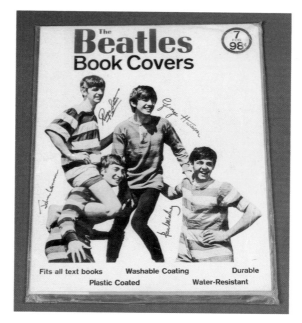

Plate 28. *Book Covers* were made by Book Covers, Inc. There are seven in the sealed package. Good, $110.00; Excellent/Mint, $120.00.

Plate 29. *Bongos* are one of the most difficult items to find. They were made by Mastro and are plastic with white skin on top. Good, $3,000.00; Excellent/Mint, $8,000.00.

Plate 30. *Bongo variation* in original Beatle Box. Good, $3,800.00; Excellent/Mint, $8,500.00.

Plate 31. *Booty Bag* is waterproof and made of clear plastic. It came with an insert that describes different uses. They can be carried in three different ways. Good, $150.00; Excellent/Mint, $165.00.

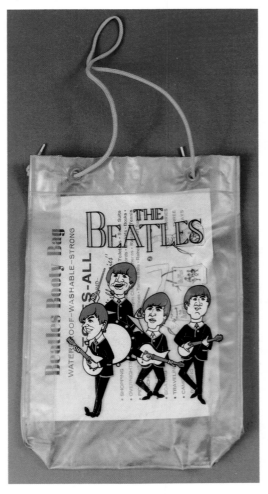

Plate 32. *Booty Bag* produced in another color variation. Good, $150.00; Excellent/Mint, $165.00.

Plate 33. *Bust* is of Ringo and was produced by Starfans. It is 6¼" tall and is made of hard rubber. There are no busts of the other Beatles. Good, $200.00; Excellent/Mint, $250.00.

Plate 34. *Bendy* was manufactured in England and Paul was the only Beatle produced. Good, $350.00; Excellent/Mint, $400.00.

Plate 35. *Bubble Bath* was produced by Colgate. Paul is 9" tall and his head unscrews to reveal contents. Good, $100.00; Excellent/Mint (in box), $500.00.

Plate 36. *Bubble Bath* utilizes Ringo. For some unknown reason, Ringo and Paul were the only two Beatles to be used by Colgate as soap containers. Good, $100.00; Excellent/Mint (in box), $500.00.

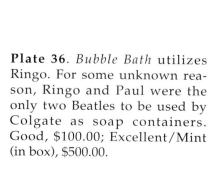

Plate 37. *Bedspread* is made of white cotton and is embroidered in six different colors. Good, $450.00; Excellent/Mint, $500.00.

Plate 38. *Beat Seats* were produced in England and are very hard to find. The ones pictured here are from the person who produced them in his factory in the 1960s. Good, $1,200.00; Excellent/Mint, $1,500.00.

Plate 39. *Beat Seats* were done in different colors for each Beatle. Good, $1,200.00; Excellent/Mint, $1,500.00.

Plate 40. *Bicycle Flags* are made of heavy plastic and are a very hard-to-find item. Good, $400.00; Excellent/Mint, $600.00.

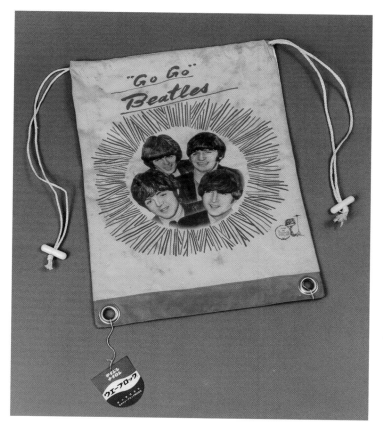

Plate 41. *GoGo Bags* were made and sold in the Japanese market. Since the last book, a warehouse find has been made. Good, $100.00; Excellent/Mint, $125.00.

Plate 42. *Bags* shown are a different variety. Good, $100.00; Excellent/Mint, $125.00.

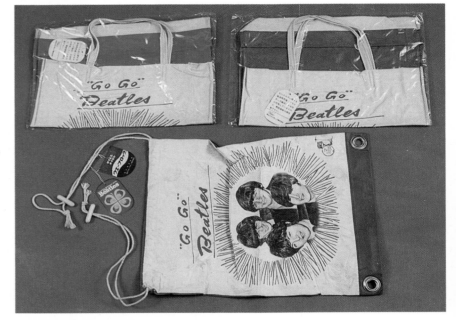

Plate 43. *Bags* shown are a different variety. Good, $100.00; Excellent/Mint, $125.00.

Plate 44. *Bags* shown are a different variety. Good, $100.00; Excellent/Mint, $125.00.

Plate 46. *Beatles Bag* is made of cloth and was used as a gym bag. Good, $2,000.00; Excellent/Mint, $2,500.00.

Plate 45. *Book Cover* was used on school books. Good, $100.00; Excellent/Mint, $125.00.

Plate 47. *Bookmark* is made of plastic. Good, $50.00; Excellent/Mint, $75.00.

Plate 48. *Butcher Cover* was a promotional poster used in the store to advertise albums. Good, $1,000.00; Excellent/Mint, $1,200.00.

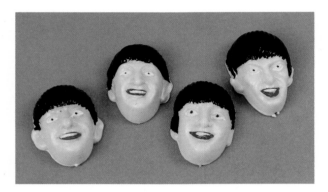

Plate 49. *Cake Decorations* are made of plastic. Good, $35.00; Excellent/Mint, $40.00.

Plate 50. *Cake Decorations* are made of plastic and can be found in a variety of sizes and poses. Good, $35.00; Excellent/Mint, $40.00.

Plate 51. *Cake Decorations* are made of paper. Good, $100.00; Excellent/Mint, $125.00.

Plate 52. *Coasters* are made of heavy duty cardboard and were used in nightclubs under drinks. Good, $50.00; Excellent/Mint, $60.00.

Plate 53. *Calendar* is a very rare item. It has plastic knobs on the back to change the date. Good, $500.00; Excellent/Mint, $550.00.

Plate 54. *Calendar* is unusual in that it was first sold in March, 1964, the first month on the calendar. Good, $150.00; Excellent/Mint, $175.00.

Plate 55. *Calendar* using "Make a Date with the Beatles" theme is very rare. It is plastic and stands upright. There are knobs on the back so one can set the day of the week, month, and date. Good, $550.00; Excellent/Mint, $600.00.

Plate 56. *Calendar Cards* were produced by Louis F. Dow Company. They are plastic and have group or individual pictures on front and specific month of 1964 – 1965 on back. Good, $40.00; Excellent/Mint, $45.00.

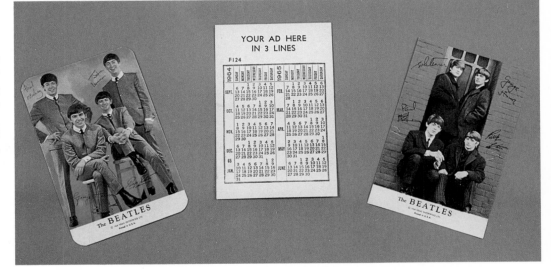

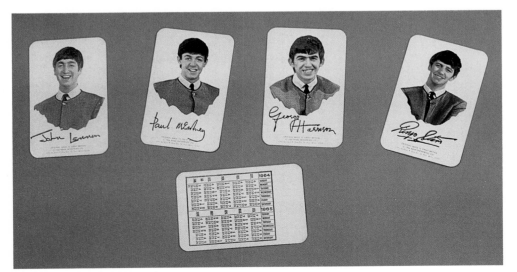

Plate 57. *Calendar Cards* were produced by Louis F. Dow Company. They are plastic and have group or individual pictures on front and specific month of 1964 – 1965 on back. Good, $40.00; Excellent/Mint, $45.00.

Plate 59. *Calendar Salesman Sample* made by Louis F. Dow Company. Calendars could be ordered with the company's logo on them. Good, $1,000.00; Excellent/Mint, $1,200.00.

Plate 58. *Calendar Salesman Sample* made by Louis F. Dow Company. Calendars could be ordered with the company's logo on them. Good, $1,000.00; Excellent/Mint, $1,200.00.

Plate 60. *Small Spiral Calendar* sold during 1964. Good, $300.00; Excellent/Mint, $325.00.

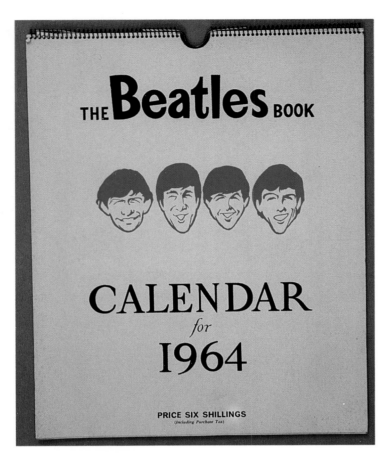

Plate 62. *Candy Dishes* were manufactured by Washington Pottery. Each is bordered with a gold trim. The Ringo dish is the only one with "The Beatles" written on the bottom. Good, $175.00; Excellent/Mint, $200.00.

Plate 61. *Large Spiral Calendar* sold for six shillings in 1964. Good, $300.00; Excellent/Mint, $325.00.

Plate 63. *Candy Cigarette Boxes* were made by World Candies, Inc. The boxes are small, measuring 1" x 2½". Each was made to hold two pieces of candy. There were many different boxes produced. Good, $110.00; Excellent/Mint, $120.00.

Plate 64. *Cap*s are known as "Ringo Caps" and are so designated on the labels inside. These Ringo Caps are brown, gray, and black. Good, $150.00; Excellent/Mint, $175.00.

Plate 65. *Cap* is another variation of the "Ringo Cap." It is made of leather. Good, $150.00; Excellent/Mint, $175.00.

Plate 66. *Cap* is another variation of the "Ringo Cap." Good, $150.00; Excellent/Mint, $175.00.

Plate 67. *Cap* is another variation of the "Ringo Cap." Good, $150.00; Excellent/Mint, $175.00.

Plate 68. *Cap* is another variation of the "Ringo Cap." Good, $150.00; Excellent/Mint, $175.00.

Plate 69. *Ringo Caps* of all different materials. Good, $150.00; Excellent/Mint, $175.00.

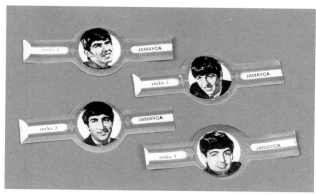

Plate 70. *Coasters* were produced in Germany. Good, $40.00; Excellent/Mint, $75.00.

Plate 71. *Cigar Bands* were made in Jamaica, thus demonstrating that the Beatles' faces were used on everything. Good, $80.00; Excellent/Mint, $90.00.

Plate 73. *Clutch Purses* were made of different materials. This one is made of vinyl and has a zippered top. Good, $225.00; Excellent/Mint, $250.00.

Plate 72. *Cigar Bands* were made in Germany. Note the names are not those of the Beatles. Good, $90.00; Excellent/Mint, $100.00.

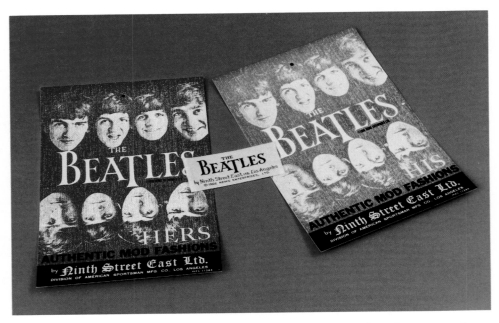

Plate 74. *Clothing Tags* were made by Ninth Street Limited and were used on mod fashion clothing. Good, $60.00; Excellent/Mint, $65.00.

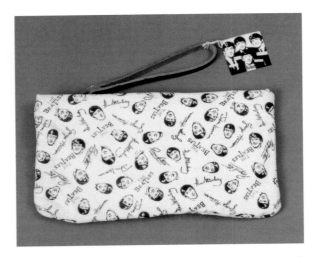

Plate 75. *Clutch Purse* is made of cloth and shows its original tag. It has a brown strap handle. Good, $300.00; Excellent/Mint, $325.00.

Plate 76. *Clutch Purse* is made of vinyl and has a zippered top with a leather-like strap. Good, $300.00; Excellent/Mint, $325.00.

Plate 77. *Clutch Purse* in a different color. Good, $350.00; Excellent/Mint, $375.00.

Plate 78. *Clutch Purse* in white color. Good, $350.00; Excellent/Mint, $375.00.

Plate 79. *Clutch Purse* in white color. Good, $350.00; Excellent/Mint, $375.00.

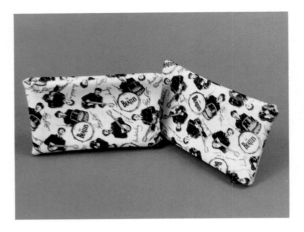

Plate 80. *Clutch Purses* are another variation utilizing different logo patterns. Good, $300.00; Excellent/Mint, $325.00.

Plate 81. *Clutch Purse* in the rare green color. Good, $350.00; Excellent/Mint, $375.00.

Plate 82. *Coin Holder Display Card*. Good, $1,000.00; Excellent/Mint, $1,200.00.

Plate 83. *Coin Purse* is made of vinyl and can be found in various colors. Good, $35.00; Excellent/Mint, $40.00.

Plate 84. *Colorforms* were made in 1966 by Colorforms. This kit utilized the Beatles and their instruments and a stage to place the pieces. A difficult toy to find in excellent condition. Good, $850.00; Excellent/Mint, $950.00.

Plate 85. *Coloring Book* was produced by Saalfield. Good, $60.00; Excellent/Mint, $75.00.

Plate 86. *Coloring Set* was manufactured by Kilfix and included five numbered portraits to be painted by the number. Good, $1,500.00; Excellent/Mint, $1,700.00.

Plate 88. *Comb* was produced by Lido Toys. It is plastic and unusually large for a comb. It measures 14½". It was produced in a variety of colors. Good, $150.00; Excellent/Mint, $200.00.

Plate 87. *Comic Book* using "Meet the Beatles" story as the main theme. Good, $50.00; Excellent/Mint, $60.00.

Plate 89. *Comic Book* using the Beatles as a story line. Good, $50.00; Excellent/Mint, $60.00.

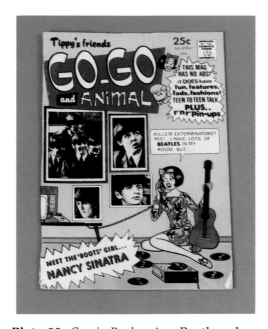

Plate 90. *Comic Book* using Beatles photographs on cover. Good, $50.00; Excellent/Mint, $60.00.

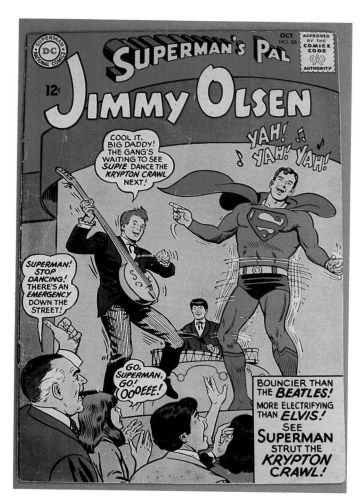

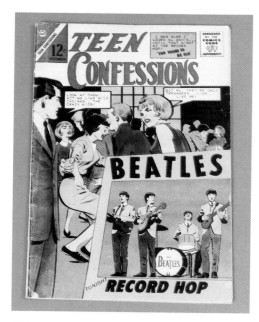

Plate 92. *Comic Book* using the Beatles as a story line. Good, $50.00; Excellent/Mint, $60.00.

Plate 91. *Comic Book*. Good, $50.00; Excellent/Mint, $60.00.

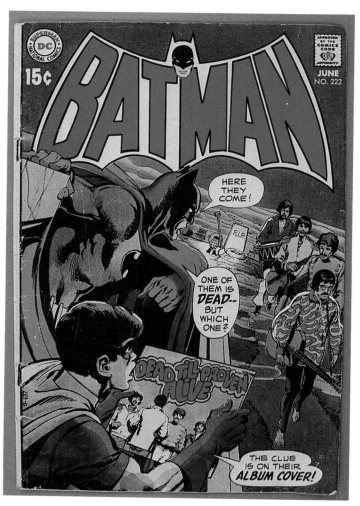

Plate 93. *Comic Book* using the Batman theme with the Beatles. Good, $50.00; Excellent/Mint, $60.00.

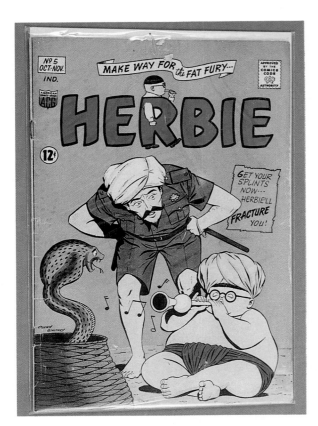

Plate 94. *Comic Book*. Good, $50.00; Excellent/Mint, $60.00.

Plate 95. *Comic Book.* Good, $50.00; Excellent/Mint, $60.00.

Plate 96. *Comic Book.* Good, $50.00; Excellent/Mint, $60.00.

Plate 97. *Compact* was made only in England and is a very rare piece of memorabilia. The one pictured has the make-up still intact. Good, $550.00; Excellent/Mint, $600.00.

Plate 98. *Corkstopper* is a very rare piece of memorabilia. The head is wooden. We have seen only John and Ringo. Good, $700.00; Excellent/Mint, $750.00.

Plate 100. *Curtains* were made in Holland demonstrating that Beatle items were produced in many countries. They are made of cloth. Good, $400.00; Excellent/Mint, $425.00.

Plate 99. *Official Beatle Cuff Links* were marked NEMS Enterprises. Good, $225.00; Excellent/Mint, $250.00.

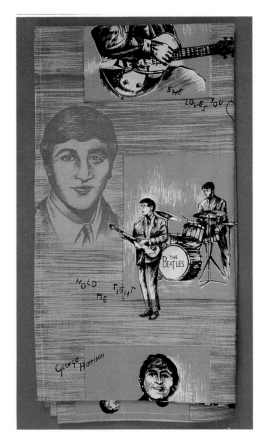

Plate 101. *Curtain variation.* Good, $400.00; Excellent/Mint, $425.00.

Plate 102. *Curtain variation.* Good, $400.00; Excellent/Mint, $425.00.

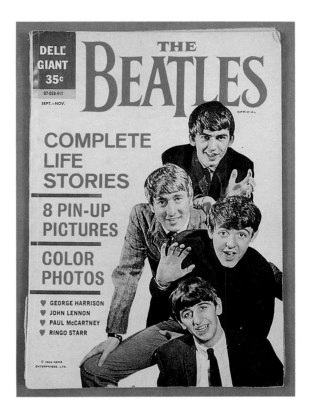

Plate 103. *Comic Book* was made by Dell and came with eight pin-up pictures. Good, $200.00; Excellent/Mint, $225.00.

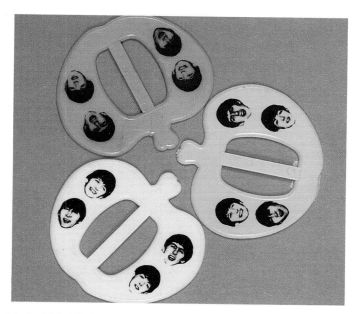

Plate 104. *Clothes tags* were made of plastic and were used in the Apple Store. Good, $25.00; Excellent/Mint, $40.00.

Plate 105. *Compact with lipstick* is the only one known to exist. The lipstick also had the Beatle identification. Good, $1,500.00; Excellent/Mint, $1,800.00.

Plate 106. *Playing Cards* were made in two variations with different header pictures. Good, $400.00; Excellent/Mint, $850.00.

Plate 107. *Playing Cards* in original box are very hard to find. Good, $850.00; Excellent/Mint, $850.00.

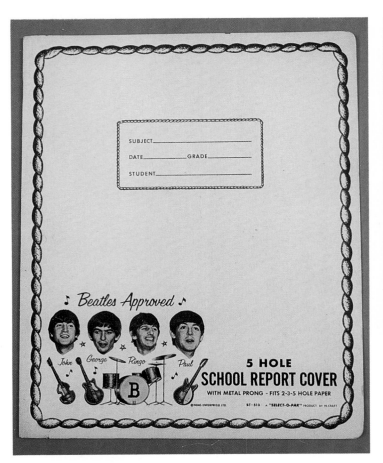

Plate 109. *Charms* used in bubble gum machine. Good, $10.00; Excellent/Mint, $15.00 (each).

Plate 108. *School Report Cover* was made by Select-O-Pak. Good, $50.00; Excellent/Mint, $75.00.

Plate 110. *Charms* on display. Card given out with a purchase of Mister Softee. Good, $200.00; Excellent/Mint, $225.00.

Plate 111. *Cup* is an example of a plastic cup distributed in the 1960s. Good, $125.00; Excellent/Mint, $150.00.

Plate 112. *Cup* is an example of a plastic cup distributed in the 1960s. Good, $125.00; Excellent/Mint, $150.00.

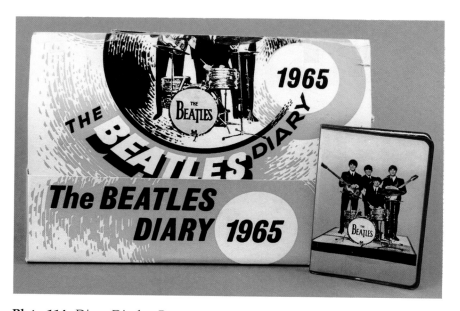

Plate 113. *Cup* with advertising. Good, $200.00; Excellent/Mint, $250.00.

Plate 114. *Diary Display Box* was used as a store display. It is one of the most common store displays. The diary was made in Scotland by the H.B. Longman Company. Good, $200.00; Excellent/Mint, $225.00.

Plate 115. *Disk Go Cases* came in nine different colors. Some are rarer and harder to find than others.

Plate 116. *Disk Go Case* in blue. Good, $150.00; Excellent/Mint, $175.00.

Plate 117. *Disk Go Case* in green. Good, $150.00; Excellent/Mint, $175.00.

Plate 118. *Disk Go Case* in pink. Good, $200.00; Excellent/Mint, $225.00.

Plate 119. *Disk Go Case* in yellow. Good, $150.00; Excellent/Mint, $175.00.

Plate 120. *Disk Go Case* in red. Good, $175.00; Excellent/Mint, $200.00.

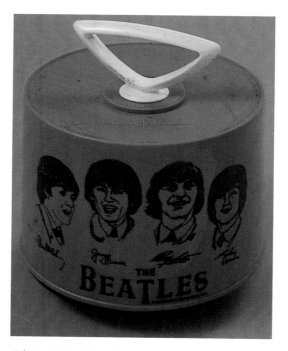

Plate 121. *Disk Go Case* in purple. Good, $175.00; Excellent/Mint, $200.00.

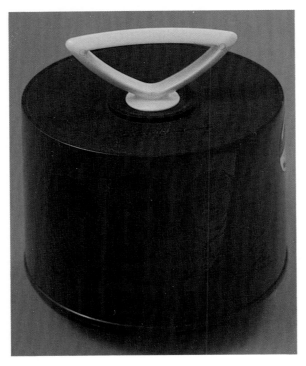

Plate 122. *Disk Go Case* in brown is by far the rarest. Good, $450.00; Excellent/Mint, $500.00.

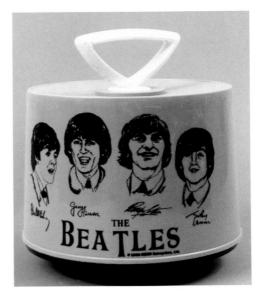

Plate 123. *Disk Go Case* in another shade of pink. Good, $150.00; Excellent/Mint, $175.00.

Plate 124. *Dolls* are of the bobbin' head variety and are in their original box. Good, $750.00; Excellent/Mint, $800.00.

Plate 125. *Dolls* are the display set of bobbin' heads. They are 14" tall and were used in stores to display smaller sets. These are among the most difficult items to find, especially as a complete set. Good, $15,000.00. Excellent/Mint, $18,000.00.

Plate 126. *Doll* 14" George. Good, $3,500.00; Excellent/Mint, $4,000.00.

Plate 127. *Doll* 14" Paul. Good, $3,500.00; Excellent/Mint, $4,000.00.

Plate 129. *Dolls* were made by Remco and are in the original boxes. Good, $500.00; Excellent/Mint, $800.00.

Plate 128. *Doll* 14" Ringo. Good, $3,500.00; Excellent/Mint, $4,000.00.

Plate 130. *Doll* referred to as the Mascot Doll. It was made by Remco and is 29" tall. It was sold with a cardboard guitar. Good, $200.00; Excellent/Mint, $225.00.

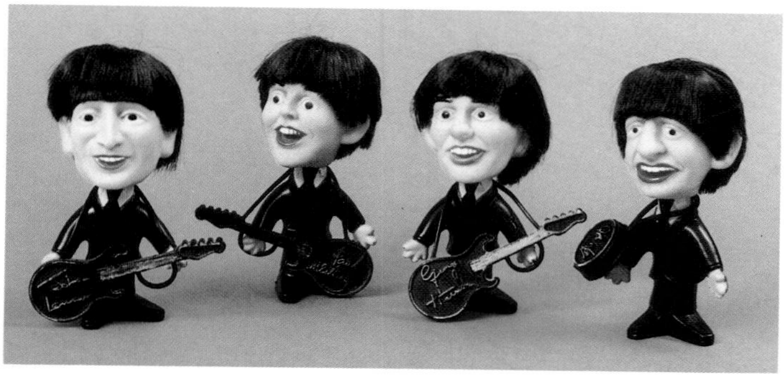

Plate 131. *Dolls* were made by the Remco Company. They are 6½" high and made of plastic. It is important that they have their instruments. Good, $375.00; Excellent/Mint, $400.00.

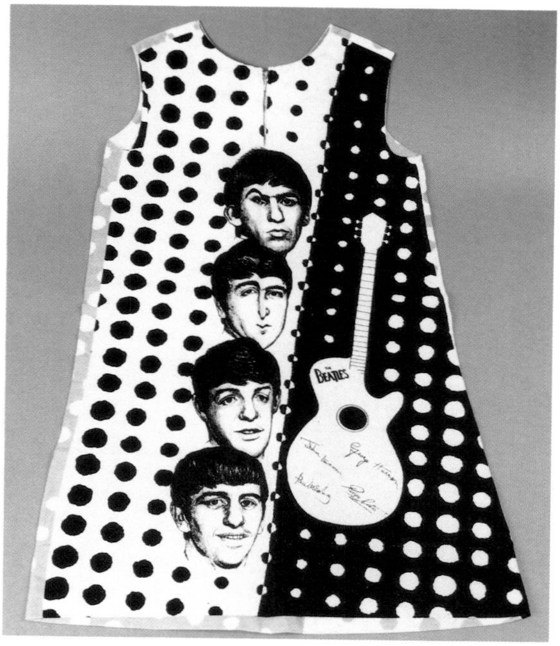

Plate 132. *Dress* was another product made in Holland. This dress shows the original label. Good, $900.00; Excellent/Mint, $1,100.00.

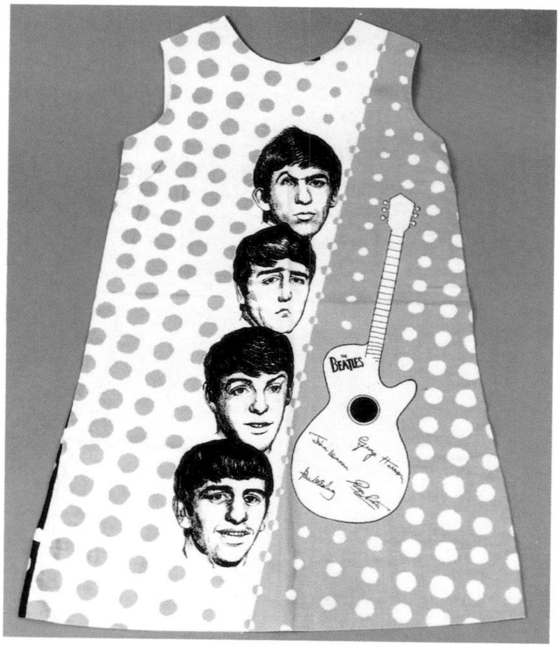

Plate 133. *Dress* shows the other side with the same pattern in blue. Good, $900.00; Excellent/Mint, $1,100.00.

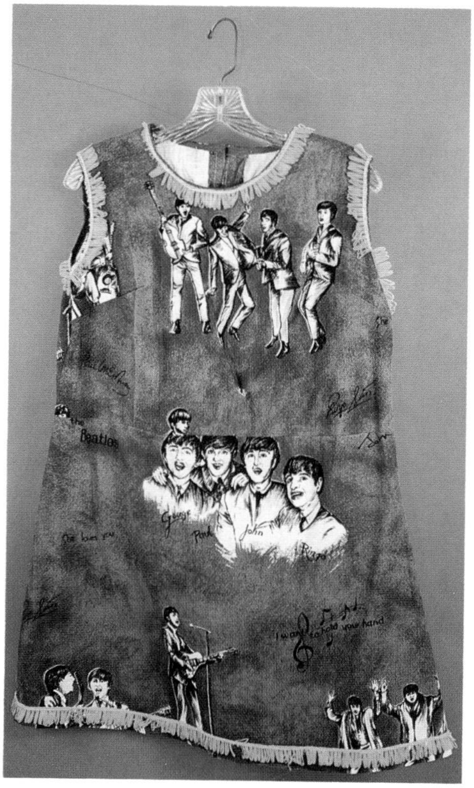

Plate 134. *Dress* shows the other side with the same pattern in green. Good, $900.00; Excellent/Mint, $1,100.00.

Plate 135. *Drum* was produced by Selcol in England. This style drum has the Ringo signature with a small face of Ringo. It is 14" wide. It is shown with original box and stand. Good, $850.00; Excellent/Mint, $900.00.

Plate 136. *Drum* is another variation of the Ringo drum. It has the large facial picture of Ringo. Good, $650.00; Excellent/Mint, $700.00.

Plate 137. *Drum* is the third variation of the Ringo Starr drum by Mastro. It utilizes only the signature on the drum. Good, $800.00; Excellent/Mint, $850.00.

Plate 138. *Drum* is made by Mastro and is the rarest variety. Good, $1,500.00; Excellent/Mint, $1,800.00.

Plate 139.

Plate 140.

Plate 141.

Plate 142.

Goebel Figurines are the rarest of all Beatles memorabilia. There are only a handful of sets known to exist. It is believed that they are prototypes because the set was never released by Goebel. Good, $3,000.00 each; Excellent/Mint, $5,000.00 each.

Plate 143. *Glasses* have the images of Beatles with musical notes on the bottom of each glass. They can be found in a variety of colors. Good, $400.00; Excellent/Mint, $425.00.

Plate 144. *Glasses* were made by J & L Company, Ltd. Each glass has a color decal and a gold rim. This set is 4" in height. Good, $450.00; Excellent/Mint, $475.00.

Plate 145. *Glasses* were produced in only the style of black faces and red notes. They are marked NEMS ENT, Ltd. London. Good, $450.00; Excellent/Mint, $500.00.

Plate 146. *Glass* is referred to as the "Dairy Queen" as it was produced in Canada and used at Dairy Queens. It is the only glass utilizing a star burst. Good, $150.00; Excellent/Mint, $175.00.

Plate 147. *Glass* was manufactured in Scotland and pictures the same photo found on diaries. Good, $200.00; Excellent/Mint, $250.00.

Plate 148. *Glass* was produced in Denmark. Good, $200.00; Excellent/Mint, $225.00.

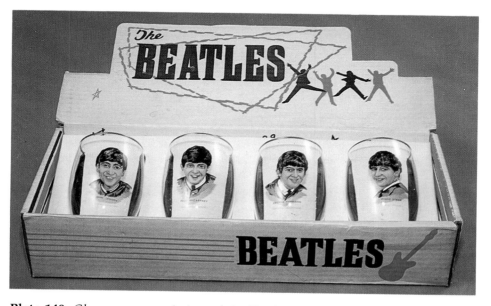

Plate 149. *Glasses* are a variation of the English set made by J & L Company. They are found in the very rare box. Good, $1,200.00; Excellent/Mint, $1,500.00.

Plate 150. *Guitar* (Four Pop) made by Mastro is 21" tall. This is the most common guitar. It was manufactured in only red and pink and is totally plastic. Good, $350.00; Excellent/Mint, $400.00.

Plate 151. *Guitar* (JR) was made by Mastro and is only 14¼", making it the smallest of the guitars. Good, $450.00; Excellent/Mint, $500.00.

Plate 152. *Guitar* (Big Six) was made by Selcol and is 33" tall. It came with six strings. Good, $500.00; Excellent/Mint, $550.00.

Plate 153. *Guitar* (New Beat) was made by Selcol and is almost identical to the Big Six except it was made with four strings. It is shown with its original coffin-shaped box. Good, $600.00; Excellent/Mint, $650.00.

Plate 154. *Guitar Box* (New Beat). Good, $200.00; Excellent/Mint, $250.00.

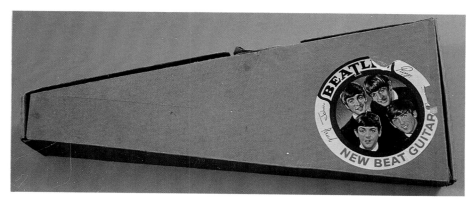

Plate 155. *Guitar Box Variation* (New Beat). Good, $300.00; Excellent/Mint, $325.00.

Plate 156. *Guitar* (New Sound) was made by Selcol. It is 23" tall and was made with four strings. Good, $500.00; Excellent/Mint, $550.00.

Plate 157. *Guitar* (English Version) referred to as a cut away. This guitar is extremely rare. Good, $1,100.00; Excellent/Mint, $1,400.00.

Plate 158. *Guitar* is a small guitar used as a jewelry box. Good, $200.00; Excellent/Mint, $225.00.

Plate 159. *Guitar* (Red Jet) is the only toy electric guitar produced. It was made by Selcol and is 31" tall. Good, $2,500.00; Excellent/Mint, $3,000.00.

Plate 160. *Guitar* (Red Jet) is a variation of this electric guitar. Good, $2,500.00; Excellent/Mint, $3,000.00.

Plate 161. *Red Jet Guitar Box*. Good, $1,000.00; Excellent/Mint, $1,200.00.

Plate 162. *Guitar* (Beatleist) was made by Mastro. It was made with six strings and is 30" tall. Good, $1,100.00; Excellent/Mint, $1,200.00.

Plate 163. *Guitar* (JNR) was made by Selcol in England. One of two guitars made with a rare paper label. Good, $3,000.00; Excellent/Mint, $3,500.00.

Plate 164. *Guitar* (Big Beat) is 21" and made by Selcol in England. Good, $1,700.00; Excellent/Mint, $2,000.00.

Plate 165. *Guitar Strings* were made by Hofner and came in a green paper container. Each package contained one guitar string. Good, $150.00; Excellent/Mint, $175.00.

Plate 166. *Gumball Fingers* are made of rubber and were placed on a display card. Good, $30.00; Excellent/Mint, $35.00.

Plate 168. *Hairbow* made by Burlington in the signature design. Good, $325.00; Excellent/Mint, $350.00.

Plate 167. *Gumball Machine* was used to vend Beatle buttons in the 1960s. Good, $600.00; Excellent/Mint, $650.00.

Plate 169. *Hairbow* produced in one of the many color variations. Good, $325.00; Excellent/Mint, $350.00.

Plate 170. *Hairbows* were made by Burlington and they came with two different logo designs. Good, $325.00; Excellent/Mint, $350.00.

Plate 171. *Hairbrush* was manufactured by Belliston Products and was produced in a variety of colors. Good, $30.00; Excellent/Mint, $35.00.

Plate 172. *Hair Dressing* is the only bottle known to exist. It was used as an aid for fine and healthy hair grooming. It was manufactured by K-G Products. Good, $1,200.00; Excellent/Mint, $1,500.00.

Plate 173. *Hair Spray* was produced by Bronson Products. The can is 8" tall and is a very sought after and hard-to-find item. Good, $900.00; Excellent/Mint, $1,200.00.

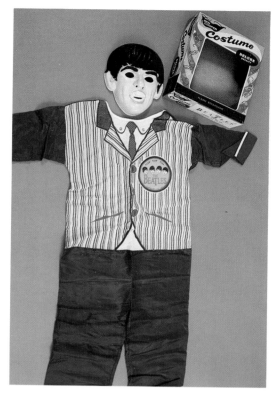

Plate 174. *Halloween Costume* made by Ben Cooper, a leading maker of Halloween costumes. It is shown with its original box. Good, $500.00; Excellent/Mint, $750.00.

Plate 175. *Halloween Costume*. Good, $500.00; Excellent/Mint, $750.00.

Plate 176. *Halloween Costume*. Good, $500.00; Excellent/Mint, $750.00.

Plate 177. *Halloween Costume*. Good, $500.00; Excellent/Mint, $750.00.

Plate 178. *Hand Puppet* came only as Ringo and there was one per large display box of candy cigarettes. Good, $500.00; Excellent/Mint, $800.00.

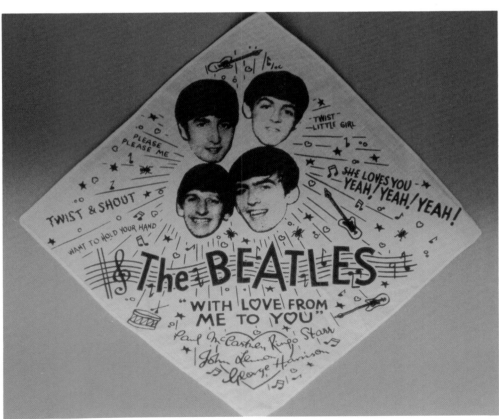

Plate 179. *Handkerchief* is made of cloth and can be found in various colors. Good, $200.00; Excellent/Mint, $215.00.

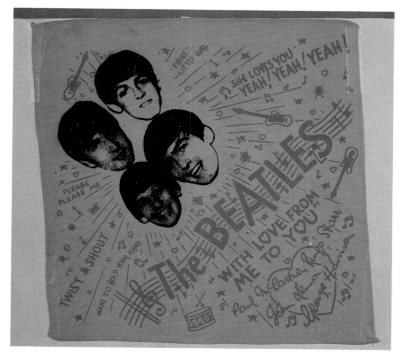

Plate 180. *Handkerchief* is made of cloth and can be found in various colors. Good, $200.00; Excellent/Mint, $215.00.

Plate 181. *Handkerchief* is made of cloth and can be found in various colors. Good, $200.00; Excellent/Mint, $215.00.

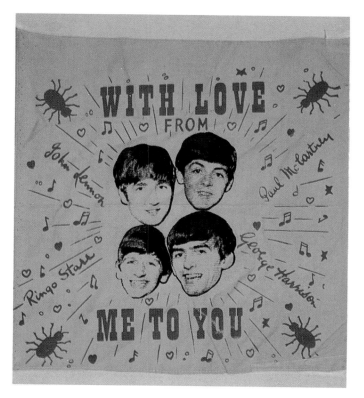

Plate 182. *Handkerchief* is made of cloth and can be found in various colors. Good, $200.00; Excellent/Mint, $215.00.

Plate 183. *Handbag* was produced in a variety of colors and handle configurations. The handles are made of brass. Good, $400.00; Excellent/Mint, $450.00.

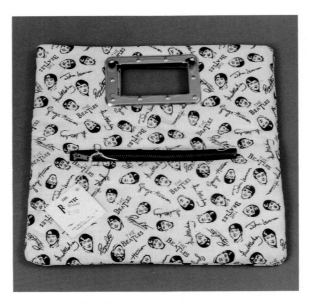

Plate 184. *Handbag* is made of vinyl and utilizes portrait and signature design. It has the original tag showing that it sold at Kesslers for $2.00. Good, $400.00; Excellent/Mint, $450.00.

Plate 185. *Hanger* was made by Saunders Ent in England. They are 16" tall and made of cardboard (John). Good, $225.00; Excellent/Mint, $250.00.

Plate 186. *Hanger*, Paul. Good, $225.00; Excellent/Mint, $250.00.

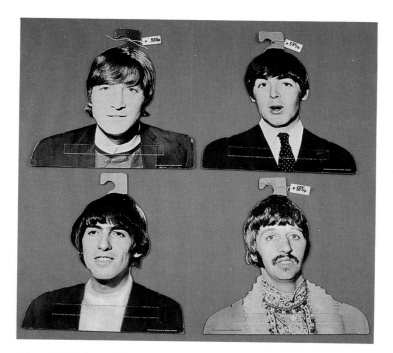

Plate 187. *Set of Hangers.* Good, $875.00; Excellent/Mint, $900.00.

Plate 188. *Hanger*, George. Good, $225.00; Excellent/Mint, $250.00.

Plate 189. *Harmonica Display* was made by Hohner and opens to show sheet music. It originally sold for $2.98. Good, $600.00; Excellent/Mint, $750.00.

Plate 190. *Harmonica Store Display* held the harmonica and sheet music combination. Good, $2,200.00; Excellent/Mint, $2,500.00.

Plate 191. *Hat* is referred to as a beach hat. It was produced in different colors. Good, $120.00; Excellent/Mint, $130.00.

Plate 192. *Hatbox* is made of vinyl by AirFlite. It was manufactured in only two colors — black and red. Good, $700.00; Excellent/Mint, $750.00.

Plate 193. *Hatbox* shows the other color variation of the AirFlite product. Good, $700.00; Excellent/Mint, $750.00.

Plate 194. *Headband* was made by Better Wear, Inc., and can be found in a variety of eight colors. Good, $70.00; Excellent/Mint, $75.00.

Plate 195. *Headband* is an Australian product made by LTC Vincent. It is a rare headband. Good, $275.00; Excellent/Mint, $300.00.

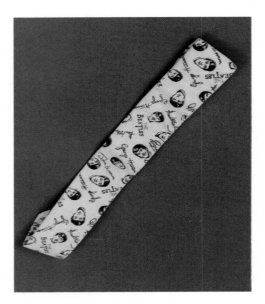

Plate 196. *Headband* is an unusual variation using faces and signature design. Good, $170.00; Excellent/Mint, $180.00.

Plate 197. *Headband* was produced by Burlington and is made of cloth. Good, $175.00; Excellent/Mint, $200.00.

Plate 198. *Headband* on original card made by Dame. Good, $175.00; Excellent/Mint, $200.00.

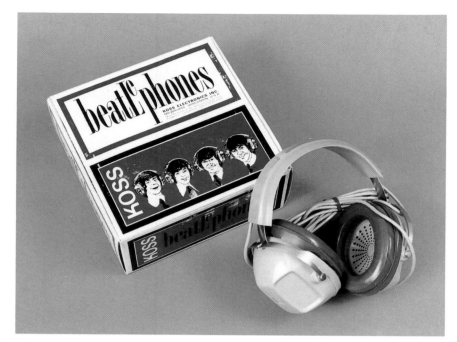

Plate 199. *Headphones* are an incredible item produced by Koss Electronics who still produce headphones today. The Beatle headphones have a sticker on each earphone. A boxed set is very difficult to find. Good, $2,500.00; Excellent/Mint, $3,000.00.

Plate 200. *Hors d'oeuvre Picks* were made in Hong Kong and flash between Beatles and hearts. Good, $115.00; Excellent/Mint, $120.00.

Plate 201. *Hummer and Hummer Box* were produced by Louis F. Dow Company. The hummer is a musical instrument made of cardboard. All of them were produced with this pattern. Good, $250.00; Excellent/Mint, $300.00.

Plate 202. *Inflatables* are made of plastic and when blown up measure 13" tall. Good, $115.00; Excellent/Mint, $135.00.

Plate 203. *Inflatable Advertisement* shown on the front of Lux soap boxes. The boxes were available in a variety of colors. Good, $400.00; Excellent/Mint, $425.00.

Plate 204. *Inflatable Advertisement* shown on Nestle's Quick Chocolate flavor tins. Good, $600.00; Excellent/Mint, $650.00.

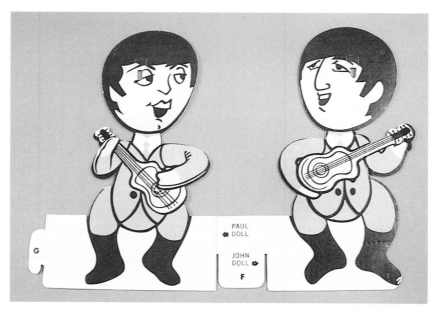

Plate 205. *Inflatable Store Display.* Good, $600.00; Excellent/Mint, $625.00.

Photo 206. *Linen* was made by Ulster and is referred to as Irish Linen. It is used as a wall hanging. Good, $175.00; Excellent/Mint, $200.00.

Plate 207. *Kaboodle Kits* were made by Standard Plastic Products. Good, $800.00; Excellent/Mint, $1,500.00.

Photo 208. *Kaboodle Kit* was manufactured by Standard Plastic Production, Inc. They were available in a variety of colors. One of the most desired Beatles collectibles. Good, $850.00; Excellent/Mint, $900.00.

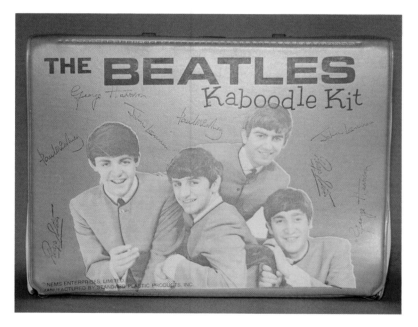

Plate 209. *Kaboodle Kit* shown in another of the color varieties. Good, $850.00; Excellent/Mint, $925.00.

Plate 210. *Lamp* was hung by a screw to the wall. The shade is paper and came without a bulb holder. Good, $600.00; Excellent/Mint, $650.00.

Plate 211. *Lamp* is a paper cylinder with wire legs so that it stands. Inside is a place for a light bulb. Good, $700.00; Excellent/Mint, $725.00.

Plate 212. *Lamp* is the rarest of the three types produced. The shade is cardboard and the base is ceramic with a gold guitar painted on it. Good, $1,100.00; Excellent/Mint, $1,200.00.

Plate 213. *Lamp variation.* Good, $850.00; Excellent/Mint, $900.00.

Plate 214. *Licorice Candy Records* were made by Clevedon Confectionery. Good, $1,500.00; Excellent/Mint, $1,600.00 (set).

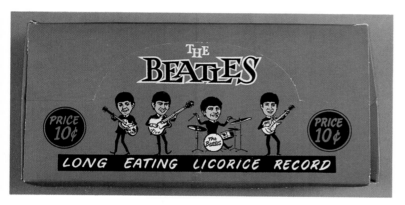

Plate 215. *Licorice Candy Record Box.* Good, $1,000.00; Excellent/Mint, $1,200.00.

Plate 216. *Litter Holder* is vinyl and made by Air-Flite. It opens up and could be used in a car for litter. Good, $300.00; Excellent/Mint, $325.00.

Plate 217. *Lunch Box* was produced by Aladdin Industries. It is made of metal and comes with the appropriate blue thermos. It is very sought-after by lunch box collectors. Good, $600.00; Excellent/Mint, $650.00.

Plate 218. *Magnetic Hairstyle Game* was produced by Merit. It is made of heavy cardboard and utilizes magnets. Good, $750.00; Excellent/Mint, $800.00.

Plate 219. *Marionette* (George) is made of wood and the maker is unknown. These individual marionettes are very rare. Good, $500.00; Excellent/Mint, $525.00.

Plate 220. *Marionette* (Ringo). Good, $500.00; Excellent/Mint, $525.00.

Plate 221. *Marionette* (John). Good, $500.00; Excellent/Mint, $525.00.

Plate 222. *Models* were made by the Revell Company, maker of many types of models. Good, $400.00; Excellent/Mint, $450.00.

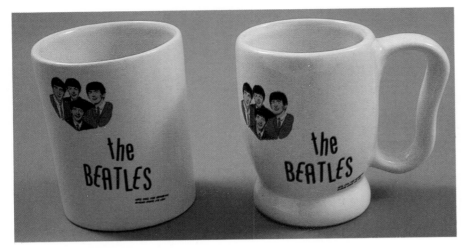

Plate 223. *Mugs* were made in Canada and are made of pottery. Good, $180.00; Excellent/Mint, $200.00.

Plate 224. *Movie* shows the Beatles at London and Kennedy Airports. Good, $200.00; Excellent/Mint, $225.00.

Plate 225. *Megaphones* were made in these three colors. Good, $850.00; Excellent/Mint, $1,000.00.

Plate 226. *Napkins* are found in their original packaging. There are a total of 50 napkins included. Good, $700.00; Excellent/Mint, $725.00.

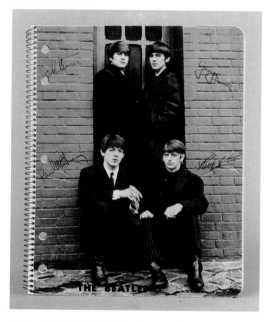

Plate 227. *Notebooks* (group) were made by Westab. This is an example of one that is spiral-bound. Good, $150.00; Excellent/Mint, $175.00.

Plate 228. *Notebook* (group) was produced by Westab. It measures 8½" x 11". This example has the binding on the side. Good, $150.00; Excellent/Mint, $175.00.

Plate 229. *Notebook* (group) shows an example of one bound at the top. Good, $100.00; Excellent/Mint, $125.00.

Plate 230. *Notebook* (group) shows another variation with three holes. Good, $100.00; Excellent/Mint, $125.00.

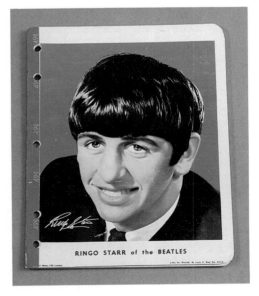

Plate 231. *Notebook* was made by Westab by Louis F. Dow & Co. Good, $200.00; Excellent/Mint, $225.00.

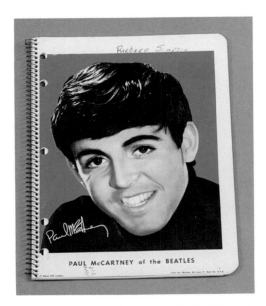

Plate 232. *Notebook* was made by Westab by Louis F. Dow & Co. Good, $200.00; Excellent/Mint, $225.00.

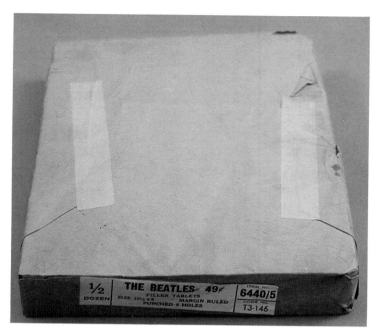

Plate 233. *Notebook Filler Tablets* in original packaging. Good, $500.00; Excellent/Mint, $750.00.

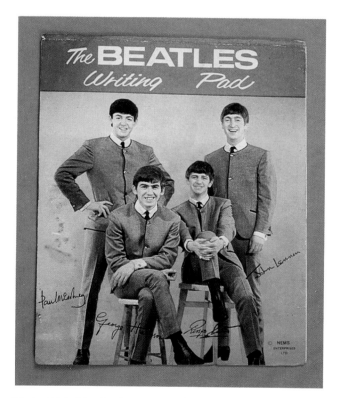

Plate 234. *Notebook* was made by Nems for English Market. Good, $300.00; Excellent/Mint, $325.00.

Plate 235. *Nylons* made by Ballito shown from the back side with the Beatles' pictures and signatures. Good, $130.00; Excellent/Mint, $140.00.

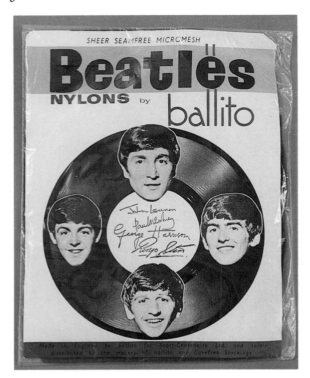

Plate 236. *Nylons* were made by Scott-Centenaire Company. This is an example of the Ballito textured mesh stockings. Good, $130.00; Excellent/Mint, $140.00.

Plate 237. *Nylons* made by Vroom & Dressman. Good, $180.00; Excellent/Mint, $200.00.

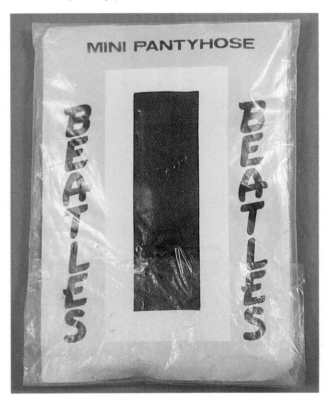

Plate 238. *Nylons* (mini pantyhose). Good, $200.00; Excellent/Mint, $225.00.

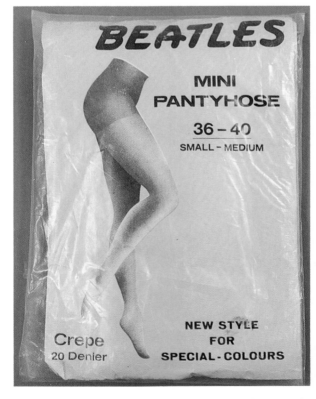

Plate 239. *Nylons* (mini pantyhose). Good, $200.00; Excellent/Mint, $225.00.

Plate 240. *Nylons Display Card* used to promote Ballito stockings in conjunction with the movie, *A Hard Day's Night*. Good, $900.00; Excellent/Mint, $1,100.00.

Plate 241. *Ornaments* were used to hang on Christmas trees. Each was hand blown, so they may vary. Good, $300.00; Excellent/Mint, $325.00.

Plate 242. *Ornaments* have the guitar in either left or right hand and that identifies which Beatle it is. Good, $300.00; Excellent/Mint, $325.00.

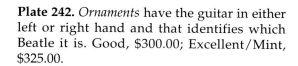

Plate 243. *Ornament* in blue. Good, $300.00; Excellent/Mint, $325.00.

Plate 244. *Ornament* in red with guitar. Good, $300.00; Excellent/Mint, $325.00.

Plate 245. *Ornament* in gold with guitar in right hand. Good, $300.00; Excellent/Mint, $325.00.

Plate 246. *Ornament* in pink with guitar in right hand. Good, $300.00; Excellent/Mint, $325.00.

Plate 247. *Paint by Number* was produced by Artistic Creations. (Paul). Good, $1,300.00; Excellent/Mint, $1,500.00.

Plate 248. *Paint by Number* was produced by Artistic Creations (Ringo). Good, $1,300.00; Excellent/Mint, $1,500.00.

Plate 249. *Paint by Number* was produced by Artistic Creations (George). Good, $1,300.00; Excellent/Mint, $1,500.00.

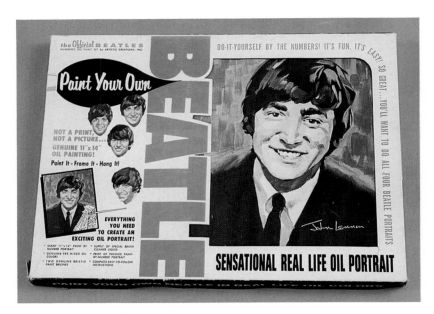

Plate 250. *Paint by Number* was produced by Artistic Creations (John). Good, $1,300.00; Excellent/Mint, $1,500.00.

Plate 251. *Paint by Number* included paints, brush, and one Beatle portrait to paint. Good, $1,300.00; Excellent/Mint, $1,500.00.

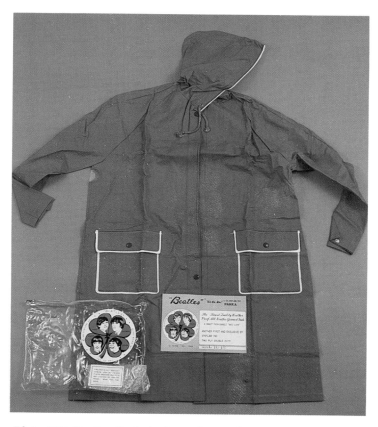

Plate 252. *Beatles Parka* is the only one known to exist and it is marked 1985 NEMS. It was made by Vinyl Lamb, Inc., and is referred to as GoGo Dri Parka. Good, $900.00; Excellent/Mint, $1,000.00.

Plate 253. *Pens* were made by the Press Initial Corporation. They were produced in many colors but all feature four heads on the pen top. Good, $175.00; Excellent/Mint, $200.00.

Plate 254. *Pens* were made by the Press Initial Corporation. They were produced in many colors but all feature four heads on the pen top. Good, $175.00; Excellent/Mint, $200.00.

Plate 255. *Pens* were made in Denmark and are very hard to find. Good, $175.00; Excellent/Mint, $200.00.

Plate 256. *Pen.* Good, $175.00; Excellent/Mint, $200.00.

Plate 257. *Pen Holder* is ceramic and made for Seltaeb. Very hard to find. Good, $1,200.00; Excellent/Mint, $1,500.00.

Plate 258. *Pencil* is from the 1960s. Good, $150.00; Excellent/Mint, $200.00.

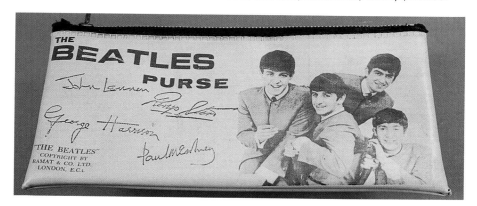

Plate 259. *Pencil Cases* were by Standard Plastic Products and are made of vinyl. Good, $175.00; Excellent/Mint, $200.00.

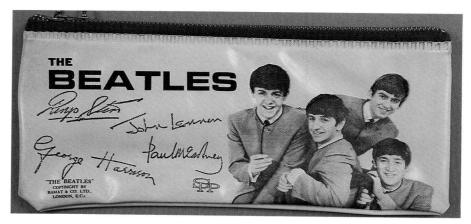

Plate 260. *Pencil Case* in the yellow color. Good, $175.00; Excellent/Mint, $200.00.

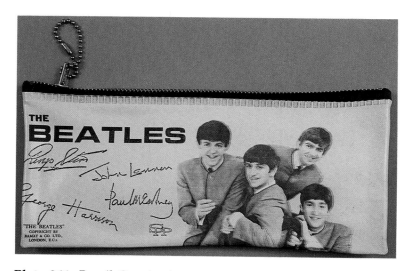

Plate 261. *Pencil Case* in the gray version. Good, $175.00; Excellent/Mint, $200.00.

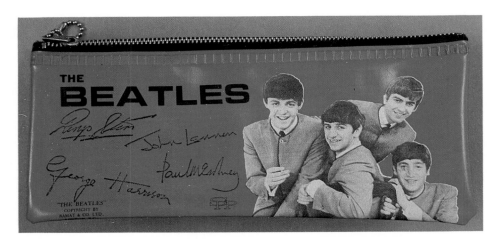

Plate 262. *Pencil Case* in red. Good, $175.00; Excellent/Mint, $200.00.

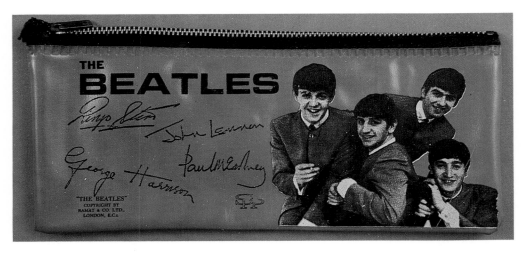

Plate 263. *Pencil Case* in turquoise. Good, $175.00; Excellent/Mint, $200.00.

Plate 264. *Purse* was copyrighted by Rama & Co. Good, $600.00; Excellent/Mint, $650.00.

Plate 265. *Purse* is made in Holland and there are only a few examples known to exist. Good, $1,000.00; Excellent/Mint, $1,200.00.

Plate 266. *Purse* is made of vinyl and uses repeating images. Good, $200.00; Excellent/Mint, $225.00.

Plate 267. *Pennant.* Good, $300.00 Excellent/Mint, $325.00.

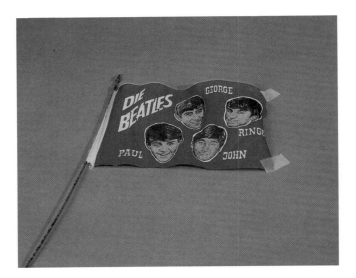

Plate 268. *Pennant.* Good, $35.00; Excellent/Mint, $40.00.

Plate 269. *Pennant* was made by Irwin Specialities. It is 22" long. Good, $250.00; Excellent/Mint, $275.00.

Plate 270. *Pennant.* Good, $40.00; Excellent/Mint, $45.00.

Plate 271. *Pennant.* Good, $175.00; Excellent/Mint, $200.00.

Plate 272. *Pennant.* Good, $100.00; Excellent/Mint, $125.00.

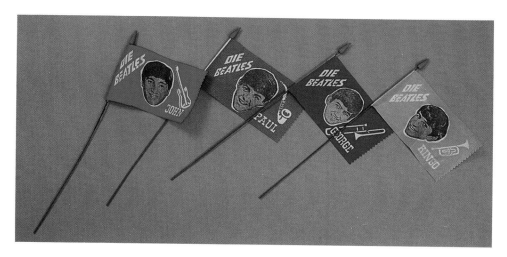

Plate 273. *Pennants.* Good, $150.00; Excellent/Mint, $175.00.

Plate 274. *Pennant.* Good, $75.00; Excellent/Mint, $100.00.

Plate 275. *Pennant.* Good, $150.00; Excellent/Mint, $175.00.

Plate 276. *Pennant.* Good, $300.00; Excellent/Mint, $325.00.

Plate 277. *Pennant.* Good, $200.00; Excellent/Mint, $225.00.

Plate 278. *Pennant.* Good, $350.00; Excellent/Mint, $375.00.

Plate 279. *Pennant.* Good, $40.00; Excellent/Mint, $45.00.

Plate 280. Pillows are the three variations made by Nordic House. 1st, Good, $200.00; Excellent/Mint, $225.00. 2nd, Good, $125.00; Excellent/Mint, $150.00. 3rd, Good, $325.00; Excellent/Mint, $350.00.

Plate 281. *Placards* came in a set of different Beatles sayings. Good, $15.00; Excellent/Mint, $20.00.

Plate 282. *Pomade* was made by H. H. Cosmetic Lab in the Philippines. The box held fifty of the small packets of hair grease. They sold originally for 10 cents each. Good, $3,500.00; Excellent/Mint, $4,000.00.

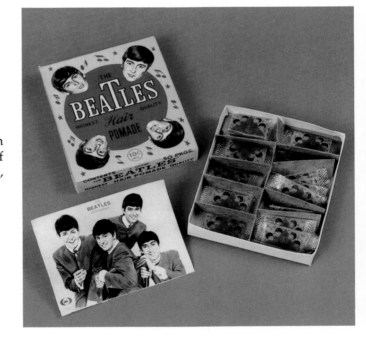

Plate 283. *Pomade Packet.* Good, $50.00; Excellent/Mint, $75.00.

Plate 284. *Portraits* (Ringo Starr) were suitable for framing. Good, $100.00; Excellent/Mint, $110.00.

Plate 285. *Portraits* (Paul). Good, $100.00; Excellent/Mint, $110.00.

Plate 286. *Portraits* (George). Good, $100.00; Excellent/Mint, $110.00.

Plate 287. *Portraits* (John). Good, $100.00; Excellent/Mint, $110.00.

Plate 288. *Portraits* included six 8" x 10 " pictures of the Beatles and were made by J.M. Distributors. Good, $115.00; Excellent/Mint, $120.00.

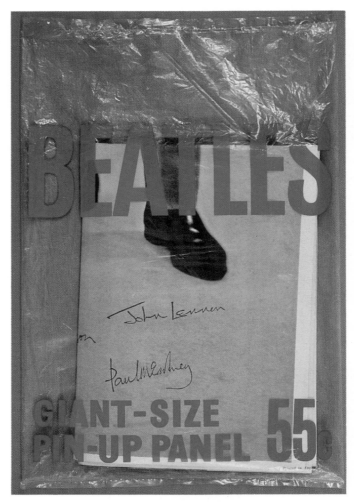

Plate 289. *Poster* was made by Dell and is 54" x 20". Good, $75.00; Excellent/Mint, $100.00.

Plate 290. *Poster* was made by Dell and is shown here in the original packaging. Good, $50.00; Excellent/Mint, $60.00.

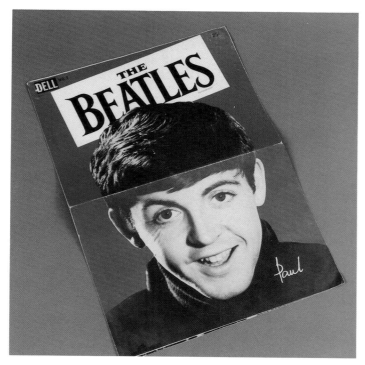

Plate 291. *Poster* was made by Dell and sold for 25 cents. Good, $50.00; Excellent/Mint, $60.00.

Plate 292. *Poster* is one of the largest made and is shown here in original mailer. It was made by PYX Products. Good, $80.00; Excellent/Mint, $90.00.

Plate 293. *Puzzle* is of the jigsaw variety and utilizes 340 pieces. Good, $300.00; Excellent/Mint, $350.00.

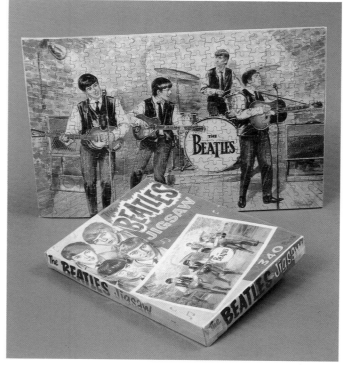

Plate 294. *Puzzle Variations.* Good, $350.00; Excellent/Mint, $400.00.

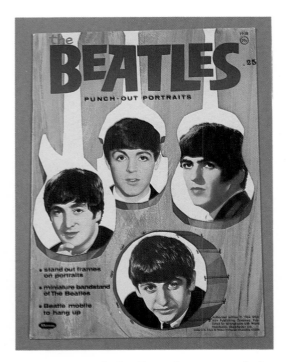

Plate 295. *Punch-Out Portraits* were made by Whitman. Good, $175.00; Excellent/Mint, $200.00.

Plate 296. *Plate* was made by Mayfair. Good, $400.00; Excellent/Mint, $450.00.

Plate 297. *Photo Promotion* given out by Mobil Oil. Good, $100.00; Excellent/Mint, $150.00.

Plate 298. *Photograph Album* is very rare. Good, $600.00; Excellent/Mint, $625.00.

Plate 299. *Portraits* were given out by Capitol Records. Good, $100.00; Excellent/Mint, $125.00.

Plate 300. *Patch* was used for jeans. Good, $50.00; Excellent/Mint, $60.00.

Plate 301. *Pants* sold in the Apple Shop shown with original tag as authentic mod fashions. Good, $300.00; Excellent/Mint, $350.00.

Plate 302. *Record Carrier* was produced by Seagull Enterprises. It can hold 45 records and utilizes plastic sleeves for the records. Good, $200.00; Excellent/Mint, $225.00.

Plate 303. *Record Carrier* was produced by Seagull Enterprises. It can hold 45 records and utilizes plastic sleeves for the records. Good, $200.00; Excellent/Mint, $225.00.

Plate 304. *Record Case* was made by AirFlite and is heavy cardboard. This model was designed to hold 33 rpm records. Good, $400.00; Excellent/Mint, $450.00.

Plate 305. *Record Player* is four-speed and has the picture of the Beatles in top half. Good, $4,000.00; Excellent/Mint, $4,800.00.

Plate 306. *Record Player* was produced in a limited quantity. The front has a Beatles sticker on the right side. Good, $4,000.00; Excellent/Mint, $4,800.00.

Plate 307. *Record Case* was made by AirFlite and used to hold 33 rpm. recordsGood, $500.00; Excellent/Mint, $650.00.

Plate 308. *Record Case* was made in Denmark and is the rarest of all record cases. Good, $550.00; Excellent/Mint $600.00.

Plate 309. *Ringo Rolls* are Life Savers using the "Ringo" name. Good, $50.00; Excellent/Mint, $75.00.

Plate 310. *Record* used as a promotion featuring the Beatles, the Beach Boys, and the Kingston Trio. Good, $500.00; Excellent/Mint, $525.00.

Plate 311. *Rug* was produced in Belgium and measures 33¼" x 32¼". Good, $400.00; Excellent/Mint, $425.00.

Plate 312. *Scarf* in the original package with original tag. It was made by Scammonden Woolen Company in England. Good, $350.00; Excellent/Mint, $375.00.

Plate 313. *Scarf* was made by Blackpool Publishers. It is 26" square. Good, $200.00; Excellent/Mint, $225.00.

Plate 314. *Scarf* is shown with original tag. It is 26" square. Good, $140.00; Excellent/Mint, $145.00.

Plate 315. *Scarf* is the same as Plate 314 but has fringe along the edge. Good, $140.00; Excellent/Mint, $145.00.

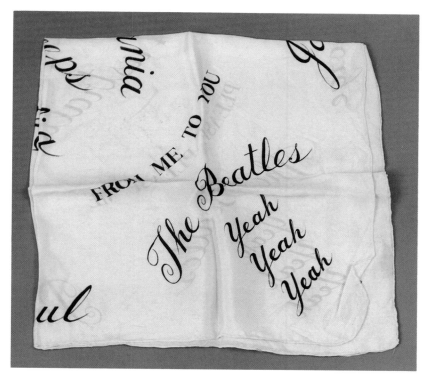

Plate 316. *Scarf* is a very rare one that was produced in Australia. Good, $200.00; Excellent/Mint, $220.00.

Plate 317. *Scarf* thought to be produced in England. It is made of cloth with leatherette straps. Good, $100.00; Excellent/Mint, $115.00.

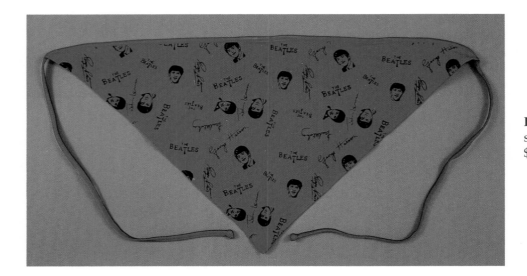

Plate 318. *Scarf* is the solid red version of the triangular scarf. Good, $100.00; Excellent/Mint, $115.00.

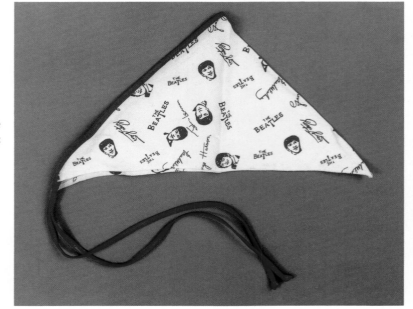

Plate 319. *Scarf* is another variation of the English triangular scarf. Good, $100.00; Excellent/Mint, $115.00.

Plate 320. *Scarf* is another variation of the English triangular scarf. Good, $100.00; Excellent/Mint, $115.00.

Plate 321. *Scarf* is a very hard one to find. Good, $250.00; Excellent/Mint, $300.00.

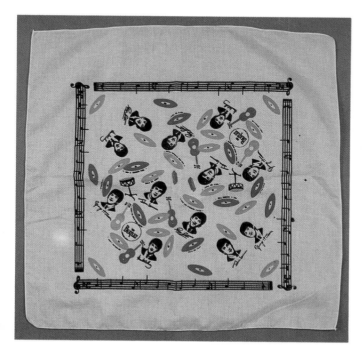

Plate 322. *Scarf.* Good, $200.00; Excellent/Mint, $225.00.

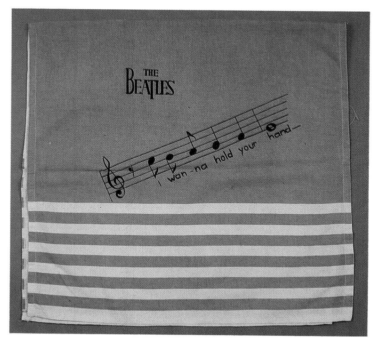

Plate 323. *Scarf.* Good, $300.00; Excellent/Mint, $350.00.

Plate 324. *Scrap Book* was made by Whitman. It originally cost 29 cents. Good, $85.00; Excellent/Mint, $95.00.

Plate 325. *Shirt* is of the knit variety. The label inside states "The only Authentic Beatle shirt." Good, $170.00; Excellent/Mint, $180.00.

Plate 326. *Sweatshirt* is made of cotton and is shown with original packaging. Good, $300.00; Excellent/Mint, $350.00.

Plate 327. *Shirt (Tee)* was made by BUD. Good, $160.00; Excellent/mint, $200.00.

Plate 328. *Splatter Toy* was made by Splatter Toy Company. Instructions were included with the toy. Good, $350.00; Excellent/Mint, $400.00.

Plate 329. *Stamps* were made by Hallmark. There were 100 stamps included. The stamps are one sheet of each Beatle and one page of a group shot. Good, $50.00; Excellent/Mint, $65.00.

Plate 330. *Stamp Banner* for store display. Good, $75.00; Excellent/Mint, $100.00.

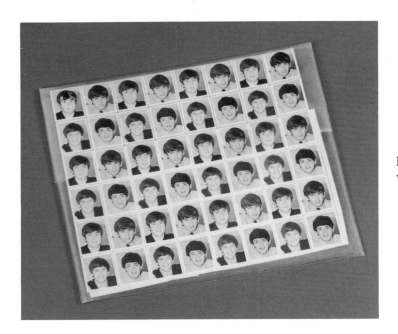

Plate 331. *Stamps* were sold in a sheet of 48 black and white stamps. Good, $50.00; Excellent/Mint, $60.00.

Plate 332. *Stamp Store Display.* Good, $270.00; Excellent/Mint, $285.00.

Plate 333. *Sunglasses* were made by Solarex. It is essential that the two stickers be in place. Good, $300.00; Excellent/Mint, $350.00.

Plate 334. *Sunglasses Store Display Banner* made by Solarex. Good, $1,000.00; Excellent/Mint, $1,100.00.

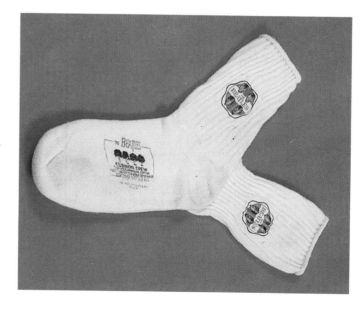

Plate 335. *Socks* shown with Beatles' emblems. Good, $400.00; Excellent/Mint, $425.00.

Plate 336. *Swingers Music Set*. Good, $150.00; Excellent/Mint, $175.00.

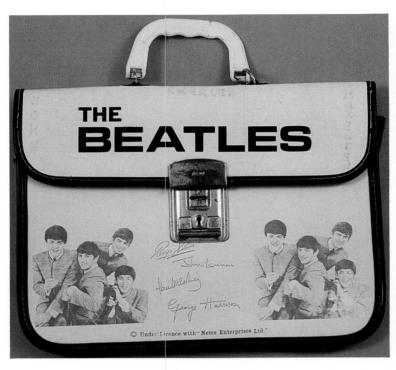

Plate 337. *School Bag* was made for the Canadian market. Good, $1,200.00; Excellent/Mint, $1,500.00.

Plate 338. *Soakys* were made by Colgate. Good, $100.00; Excellent/Mint, $400.00.

Plate 339. *Soaky* in another variation. Good, $100.00; Excellent/Mint, $400.00.

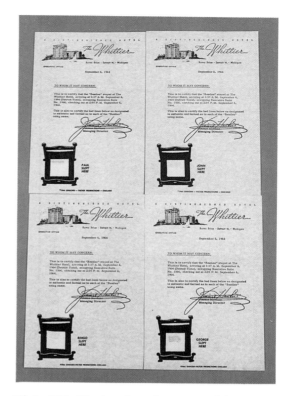

Plate 340. *Sheets* taken from actual linen the Beatles slept on at the Whittier Hotel. Good, $300.00; Excellent/Mint, $400.00.

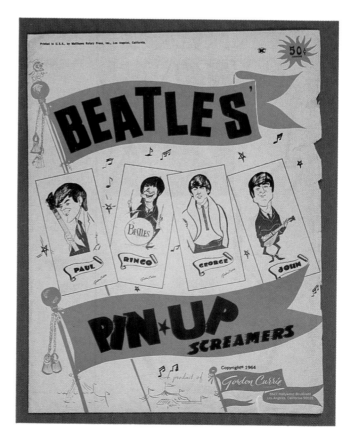

Plate 341. *Screamers* were produced by Gordon Currie. Good, $150.00; Excellent/Mint, $200.00.

Plate 342. *Ringo.* Good, $25.00; Excellent/Mint, $50.00.

Plate 343. *George.* Good, $25.00; Excellent/Mint, $50.00.

Plate 344. *Paul.* Good, $25.00; Excellent/Mint, $50.00.

Plate 345. *John.* Good, $25.00; Excellent/Mint, $50.00.

Plate 346. *Swingers Music Set.* Good, $60.00; Excellent/Mint, $70.00.

Plate 347. *Swingers Music Set.* Good, $100.00; Excellent/Mint, $125.00.

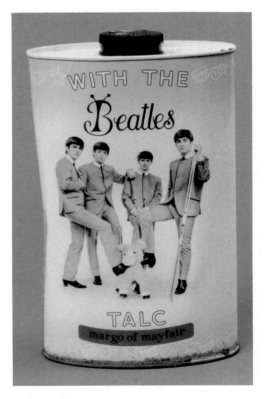

Plate 348. *Talc* was made by Margo of Mayfair. It is 7" tall. Good, $500.00; Excellent/Mint, $550.00.

Plate 349. *Tennis Shoes* were manufactured by Wing Dings. This is the low cut variety. Good, $600.00; Excellent/Mint, $650.00.

Plate 350. *Tennis Shoes* are the rarer blue variety produced by Wing Dings. Good, $650.00; Excellent/Mint, $700.00.

Plate 351. *Tennis Shoes* are the rarest high top variety. They were also made by Wing Ding. Good, $1,000.00; Excellent/Mint, $1,200.00.

Plate 352. *Ticket* used for Suffolk Downs with letter of authenticity. Good, $150.00; Excellent/Mint, $200.00.

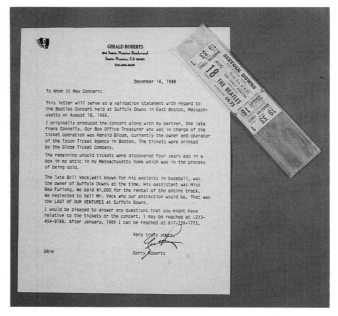

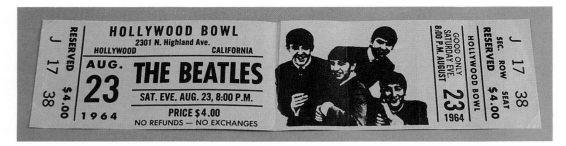

Plate 353. *Ticket* to Hollywood Bowl. Good, $150.00; Excellent/Mint, $200.00.

Plate 354. *Tile* is the most difficult to find showing all the Beatles. Good, $250.00; Excellent/Mint, $275.00.

Plate 355. *Tiles.* They are each 6" x 6" and ceramic. They are marked on the back. (George, Ringo, John). Good, $225.00; Excellent/Mint, $250.00.

Plate 356. *Back of the tiles.* Good, $225.00; Excellent/Mint, $250.00.

Plate 357. *Trading Cards* (Color Photo Box) contained 24 packs of colorized trading cards. Good, $700.00; Excellent/Mint, $725.00.

Plate 359. *Trading Cards* (Color Series Rack Pack) contained three packs of 10 cards each. Header card is essential. Good, $200.00; Excellent/Mint, $225.00.

Plate 358. *Trading Cards* (*A Hard Day's Night* Movie Box) contained 24 packs of black and white cards with scenes from the movie. Good, $650.00; Excellent/Mint, $675.00.

Plate 360. *Trading Cards* (*A Hard Day's Night* Rack Pack). Good, $200.00; Excellent/Mint, $225.00.

Plate 361. *Trading Cards* (New Series) held 24 packs of new series cards. Box top flips for use in stores. Good, $700.00; Excellent/Mint, $725.00.

Plate 362. *Trading Cards* (*A Hard Day's Night* Pack) contained five trading cards. Good, $45.00; Excellent/Mint, $50.00.

Plate 363. *Trading Cards* (Black and White Series Wrapper) made by the A & BC Company and contained black and white autographed cards. Good, $100.00; Excellent/Mint, $110.00.

Plate 364. *Trading Cards* is another series of Bubble Gum and cards. Good, $725.00; Excellent/Mint, $750.00.

Plate 365. *Trays* were made by Worcester Ware. There was a reproduction so the label on the back authenticates the piece. Good, $100.00; Excellent/Mint, $125.00.

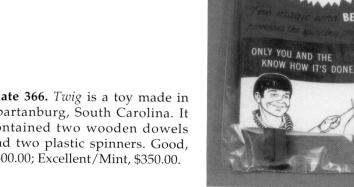

Plate 366. *Twig* is a toy made in Spartanburg, South Carolina. It contained two wooden dowels and two plastic spinners. Good, $300.00; Excellent/Mint, $350.00.

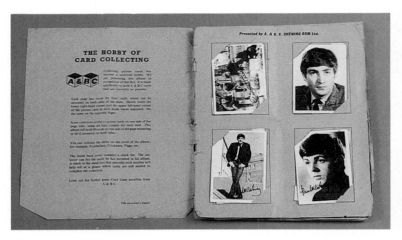

Plate 367. *Trading Card A.B.C. Chewing Gum Book.* Good, $100.00; Excellent/Mint, $120.00.

Plate 368. *Tip Tray* also referred to as Loot Tray is one of the hardest to find and most desirable items. Good, $1,500.00; Excellent/Mint, $1,800.00.

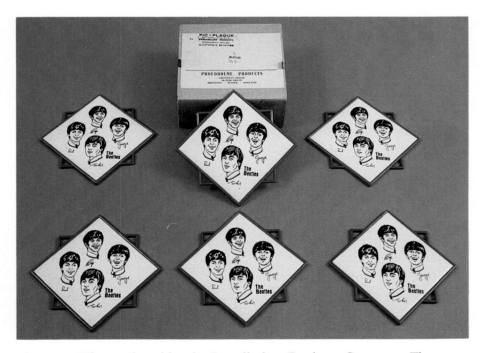

Plate 369. *Tiles* produced by the Proudholme Products Company. They came six to a carton. Good, $550.00; Excellent/Mint, $600.00.

Plate 370. *Tape* (cellophane) was made in San Juan by the Starlight Company. This was not shown to exist until March, 1992. Good, $600.00; Excellent/Mint, $625.00.

Plate 371. *Tape* (cellophane) is the smaller version. Good, $600.00; Excellent/Mint, $625.00.

Plate 372. *Towel* was made by Cannon. Good, $150.00; Excellent/Mint, $160.00.

Plate 373. *TOP STARS Bubble Gum* contained pictures of 1960s groups including the Beatles. Good, $400.00; Excellent/Mint, $450.00.

Plate 374. *Travel Bag* is made of cloth. Good, $175.00; Excellent/Mint, $200.00.

Plate 375. *Tapestry* is very colorful and the only one ever seen. Good, $500.00; Excellent/Mint, $550.00.

Plate 376. *Vanity Set* is the only one known to exist. Good, $2,000.00; Excellent/Mint, $2,200.00.

Plate 377. *Wallet* was made by Standard Plastic Products. Sold with the wallet were a nail file and a comb. Good, $130.00; Excellent/Mint, $135.00.

Photo 378. *Wallet* shown in its original packaging. This wallet came with key holder, change purse, mirror, comb, picture holder and emery board. Good, $500.00; Excellent/Mint, $700.00.

Plate 379. *Wallet* was another type that was sold. Good, $195.00; Excellent/Mint, $215.00.

Plate 381. *Wallet* in the very hard-to-find black variation. Good, $200.00; Excellent/Mint, $225.00.

Plate 380. *Wallet Dollars* were placed in these plastic holders for use in gumball machines. Good, $30.00; Excellent/Mint, $35.00.

Plate 382. *Wallpaper* was sold in rolls measuring 21" x 21". This is a piece of one of the panels. Good, $225.00; Excellent/Mint, $250.00.

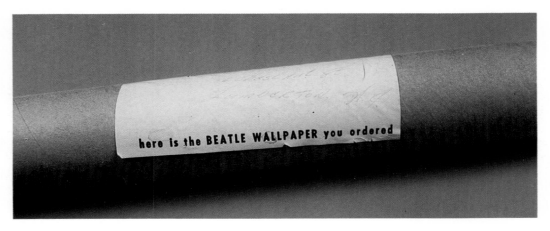

Plate 383. *Wallpaper Mailing Tube.* Good, $250.00; Excellent/Mint, $265.00.

Plate 384. *Wig* was made by Lowell Toy Manufacturing Corporation. Good, $115.00; Excellent/Mint, $125.00.

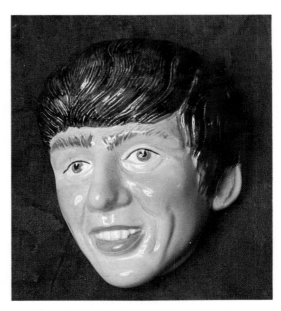

Plate 385. *Wall Plaque* was produced by Kelsbro Ware (UK) and is a ceramic head. Good, $550.00; Excellent/Mint, $600.00.

CHAPTER TWO

Jewelry

The number of different Beatles jewelry pieces produced is incredible. Most came on their own display cards which increase their values substantially. In many cases the display cards were done in both black and white and color variations.

Unknown jewelry pieces are turning up in the marketplace constantly. It is apparent that variations of many of the pieces were made in different countries.

Plate 386. *Beatles Picture Disk Necklace on card.* Good, $150.00; Excellent/Mint, $175.00.

Plate 387. *Nicky Byrne Photo Locket on card.* Good, $200.00; Excellent/Mint, $225.00.

Plate 388. *Nicky Byrne Photo Necklace on card.* Good, $225.00; Excellent/Mint, $250.00.

Plate 389. *Nicky Byrne Picture Bracelet on card.* Good, $150.00; Excellent/Mint, $175.00.

Plate 390. *Nicky Byrne Charm Bracelet on card.* Good, $175.00; Excellent/Mint, $200.00.

Plate 391. *Beatles Bracelet* by Nicky Byrne Good, $175.00; Excellent/Mint, $200.00.

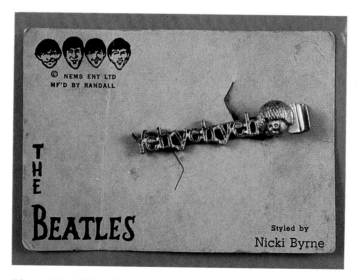

Plate 392. *Nicky Byrne Tie Clasp on card.* Good, $150.00; Excellent/Mint, $175.00.

Plate 394. *Key Chain.* Good, $50.00; Excellent/Mint, $75.00.

Plate 393. *Beatles Necklace* by Nicky Byrne. Good, $150.00; Excellent/Mint, $225.00

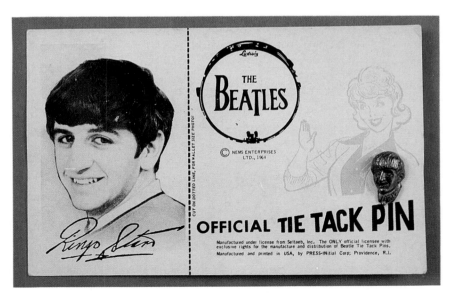

Plate 395. *Ringo Tie Tack Pin.* Good, $75.00; Excellent/Mint, $100.00.

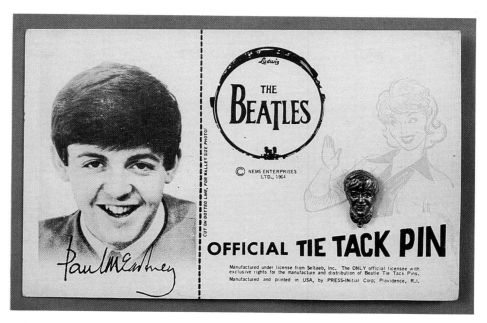

Plate 396. *Paul Tie Tack Pin.* Good, $75.00; Excellent/Mint, $100.00.

Plate 397. *Jewelry Brooch* (Pink). Good, $175.00; Excellent/Mint, $200.00.

Plate 398. *Jewelry Brooch* (John). Good, $125.00; Excellent/Mint, $150.00.

Plate 399. *Heart Necklace* by Randall. Good, $150.00; Excellent/Mint, $175.00.

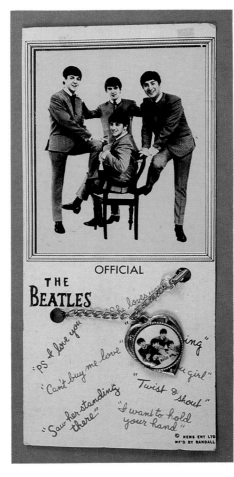

Plate 400. *Yeh Yeh Yeh Necklace* by Randall. Good, $150.00; Excellent/Mint, $175.00.

Plate 401. *Leather Jewelry Accessory.* Good, $175.00; Excellent/Mint, $200.00.

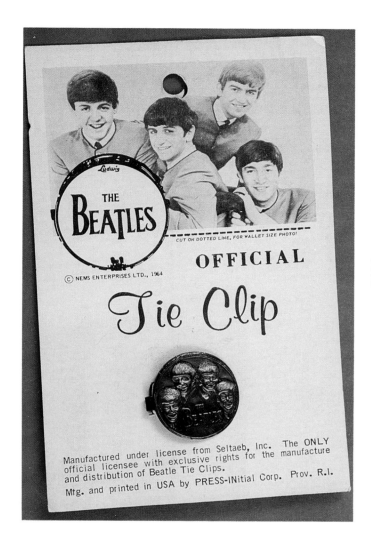

Plate. 402. *Tie Clip* by Press-Initial Corp. Good, $150.00; Excellent/Mint $175.00.

Plate 403. *Tie Tack Pin* (George). Good, $75.00; Excellent/Mint, $100.00.

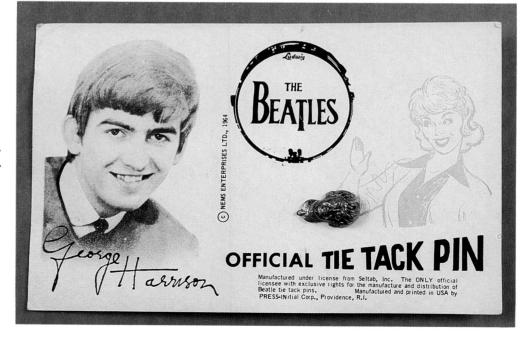

Plate 404. *Tie Tack Pins Set.* Good, $100.00; Excellent/Mint, $125.00.

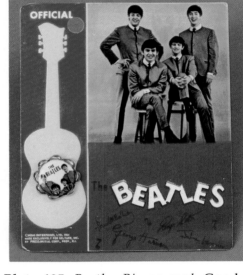

Plate 405. *Beatles Pin on card.* Good, $150.00; Excellent/Mint, $175.00.

Plate 406. *Tie Tack Pin* (guitar). Good, $125.00; Excellent/Mint, $150.00.

Plate 407. *Leather Identification Bracelet.* Good, $150.00; Excellent/Mint, $175.00.

Plate 408. *Leather Identification Bracelet.* Good, $150.00; Excellent/Mint, $175.00.

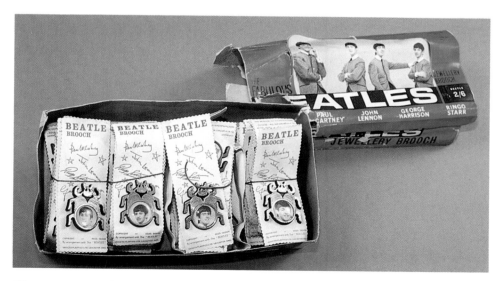

Plate 409. *Jewelry Brooches* (24) *and box.* Good, $1,200.00; Excellent/Mint, $1,500.00.

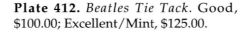

Plate 410. *Beatles Necklace.* Good, $150.00;
Excellent/Mint, $175.00.

Plate 411. *Beatles Tac on card.* Good, $150.00;
Excellent/Mint, $175.00.

Plate 412. *Beatles Tie Tack.* Good,
$100.00; Excellent/Mint, $125.00.

Plate 414. *Beatle Ring.* Good, $75.00; Excellent/Mint, $100.00.

Plate 413. *Tie Tack Pin.* Good, $75.00; Excellent/Mint, $100.00.

Plate 415. *Necklace with Pearl.* Good, $175.00; Excellent/Mint, $200.00.

Plate 416. *Paul Necklace.* Good, $75.00; Excellent/Mint, $100.00.

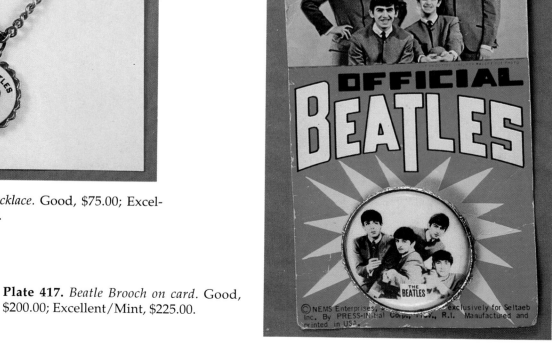

Plate 417. *Beatle Brooch on card.* Good, $200.00; Excellent/Mint, $225.00.

Plate 419. *Photo Locket.* Good, $100.00; Excellent/Mint, $115.00.

Plate 418. *Photo Locket.* Good, $100.00; Excellent/Mint, $115.00.

Plate 420. *Beatle Silver Brooch.* Good, $125.00; Excellent/Mint, $140.00.

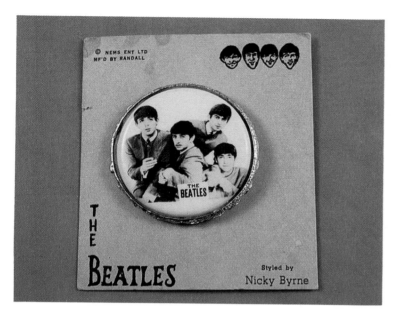

Plate 421. *Nicky Byrne Brooch on card.* Good, $175.00; Excellent/Mint, $200.00.

Plate 422. *Necklace.* Good, $100.00; Excellent/Mint, $115.00.

Plate 423. *Guitar Key Chain.* Good, $100.00; Excellent/Mint, $115.00.

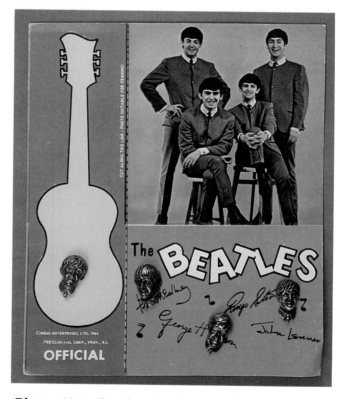

Plate 424. *Beatle Tie Tacks.* Good, $100.00; Excellent/Mint, $125.00.

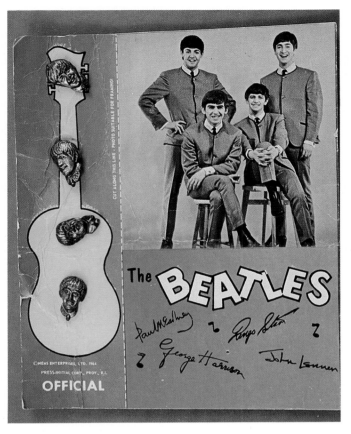

Plate 425. *Beatle Tie Tacks.* Good, $100.00; Excellent/Mint, $125.00.

Plate 426. *Key Chain.* Good, $75.00; Excellent/Mint, $100.00.

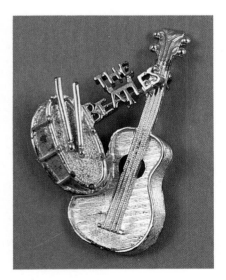

Plate 427. *Beatles Instruments Pin.* Good, $75.00; Excellent/Mint, $100.00.

Plate 428. *Beatle Brooch on card.* Good, $175.00; Excellent/Mint, $200.00.

Plate 430. *Necklace.* Good, $75.00; Excellent/Mint, $100.00.

Plate 429. *Lariat Tie.* Good, $225.00; Excellent/Mint, $250.00.

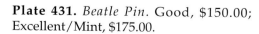

Plate 431. *Beatle Pin.* Good, $150.00; Excellent/Mint, $175.00.

Plate 432. *Guitar Pin.* Good, $150.00; Excellent/Mint, $175.00.

Plate 434. *Photo Bracelet.* Good, $75.00; Excellent/Mint, $100.00.

Plate 433. *Flasher Necklace.* Good, $75.00; Excellent/Mint, $100.00.

Plate 435. *Beatle Pin.* Good, $125.00; Excellent/Mint, $150.00.

Plate 436. *Photo Pin and Necklace.* Good, $125.00; Excellent/Mint, $150.00.

Plate 437. *Beatle Necklace.* Good, $75.00; Excellent/Mint, $100.00.

Plate 439. *Beatles Stick Pin.* Good, $50.00; Excellent/Mint, $75.00.

Plate 438. *Beatles Pin.* Good, $75.00; Excellent/Mint, $100.00.

Plate 440. *Beatles "B" Pin.* Good, $185.00;   Excellent/Mint, $200.00.

Plate 441. *Beatles Bracelet.* Good, $150.00; Excellent/Mint, $160.00.

Plate 442. *Beatles Bracelet.* Good, $150.00; Excellent/Mint, $160.00.

Plate 443. *Beatles Bracelet.* Good, $200.00; Excellent/Mint, $220.00.

Plate 444. *Beatles Flasher Ring.* Good, $50.00; Excellent/Mint, $75.00.

Plate 445. *Beatles Pin.* Good, $180.00; Excellent/Mint, $195.00.

Plate 446. *Beatles Pin.* Good, $110.00; Excellent/Mint, $115.00.

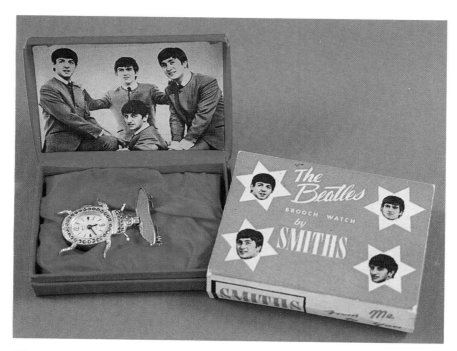

Plate 447. *Smith Watch in original box.* Good, $1,000.00; Excellent/Mint, $1,200.00.

Plate 448. *Beatles Bracelet.* Good, $150.00; Excellent/Mint, $170.00.

Plate 449. *Beatles Necklace.* Good, $150.00; Excellent/Mint, $160.00.

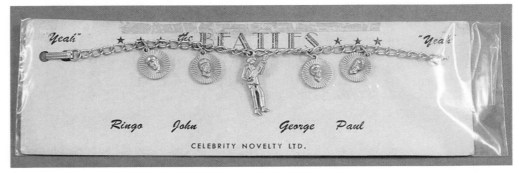

Plate 450. *Beatles Bracelet* by Celebrity Novelty. Good, $125.00; Excellent/Mint, $150.00.

Plate 451. *Beatles Bracelet.* Good, $125.00; Excellent/Mint, $150.00.

Plate 452. *Beatles Brooch.* Good, $125.00; Excellent/Mint, $135.00.

Plate 453. *Beatles Guitar Brooch.* Good, $125.00; Excellent/Mint, $135.00.

CHAPTER THREE
Buttons

Pin back buttons were produced in the United States and in England. They are grouped based on their size. The gum-ball machine buttons are 1" , the flasher buttons are 2½", and the picture or slogan buttons are 3½".

Plate 454. *Button Display* that was put on gumball machine. Good, $75.00; Excellent/Mint, $100.00.

Plate 455. *Button Store Display* used to sell buttons. Good, $200.00; Excellent/Mint, $250.00.

Plate 456. *Button Store Display.* Good, $200.00; Excellent/Mint, $250.00.

Plate 457. *Flip-Button Store Display* was used for flasher buttons. Good, $550.00; Excellent/Mint, $650.00. Flasher card. Good, $125.00; Excellent/Mint, $150.00.

Plate 458. *Buttons.* Good, $15.00; Excellent/Mint, $20.00.

Plate 459. *Buttons.* Good, $15.00; Excellent/Mint, $20.00.

Plate 461. *I Like Beatles Flasher Button.* Good, $30.00; Excellent/Mint, $35.00.

Plate 460. *Beatles Booster Button.* Good, $35.00; Excellent/Mint, $40.00.

Plate 462. *Buttons.* Good, $20.00; Excellent/Mint, $25.00.

Plate 463. *Buttons.* Good, $20.00; Excellent/Mint, $25.00.

Plate 464. *Buttons.* Good, $20.00; Excellent/Mint, $25.00.

Plate 465. *Buttons.* Good, $20.00; Excellent/Mint, $25.00.

Plate 466. *Buttons.* Good, $20.00; Excellent/Mint, $25.00.

Plate 467. *Buttons.* Good, $20.00; Excellent/Mint, $25.00.

Plate 468. *Big Button.* Good, $20.00; Excellent/Mint, $25.00.

Plate 469. *Radio Promo Button.* Good, $35.00; Excellent/Mint, $40.00.

Plate 470. *Flasher Buttons.* Good, $40.00; Excellent/Mint, $45.00.

Plate 471. *Button.* Good, $55.00; Excellent/Mint, $60.00.

Plate 472. *Large Button.* Good, $60.00; Excellent/Mint, $65.00.

Plate 473. *Beatles Fan Buttons.* Good, $35.00; Excellent/Mint, $40.00.

Plate 474. *Buttons.* Good, $20.00; Excellent/Mint, $25.00.

Plate 475. *Buttons.* Good, $20.00; Excellent/Mint, $25.00.

Plate 476. *Buttons.* Good, $20.00; Excellent/Mint, $25.00.

Plate 477. *Beatle Button Set.* Good, $125.00; Excellent/Mint, $150.00.

Plate 478. *Movie Button.* Good, $35.00; Excellent/Mint, $40.00.

Plate 479. *Love Buttons.* Good, $45.00; Excellent/Mint, $50.00.

Plate 480. *Beatle Booster Button.* Good, $75.00; Excellent/Mint, $100.00.

Plate 481. *Key Chain Flasher Button.* Good, $60.00; Excellent/Mint, $65.00.

Plate 482. *Buttons Galore.* No price.

CHAPTER FOUR

Yellow Submarine

In 1968, the Beatles completed their animated feature "Yellow Submarine." This gave them another marketing licensing bonanza. A whole new array of merchandise was produced to immortalize the movie. Cartoon characters like the Blue Meanie and Jeremy the Boob were utilized to produce different and new items.

The Yellow Submarine memorabilia is coveted today because of its vibrant colors and exciting images.

Plate 483. *Alarm Clock* was produced by Sheffield Watch Company. It is very hard to find in working order. Good, $900.00; Excellent/Mint, $1,500.00.

Plate 484. *Banks* were made by Pride Creations. They are marked with a sticker on the bottom of each figure. They are about 8" tall. Good, $2,500.00; Excellent/Mint, $3,000.00.

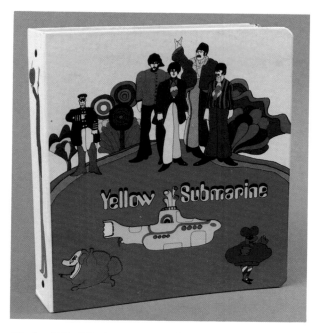

Plate 485. *Binder* was made by Vernon Royal. This was the only style binder created. Good, $325.00; Excellent/Mint, $350.00.

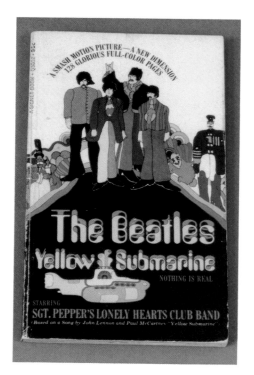

Plate 486. *Book* was published by Signet and is a paperback book. Good, $5.00; Excellent/Mint, $10.00.

Plate 487. *Bulletin Board* which is the hardest to find is pictured here showing all the Beatles. Good, $300.00; Excellent/Mint, $350.00.

Plate 488. *Buttons* made with Yellow Sub sayings. Good, $10.00; Excellent/Mint, $12.00.

Plate 489. *Buttons.* Good, $8.00; Excellent/Mint, $10.00.

Plate 490. *Buttons* with Yellow Sub images. Good, $12.00; Excellent/Mint, $15.00.

Plate 491. *Bubble Gum Wrapper* from the English set of Anglo Bubble Gum that came with a small picture. Good, $225.00; Excellent/Mint, $250.00

Plate 492. *Yellow Submarine Bike* was made by Huffy for girls. It is the rarest of the Yellow Submarine merchandise. Good, $3,200.00; Excellent/Mint, $4,500.00.

Plate 493. *Yellow Submarine Bike* was made by Huffy for girls. It is the rarest of the Yellow Submarine merchandise. Good, $3,200.00; Excellent/Mint, $4,500.00.

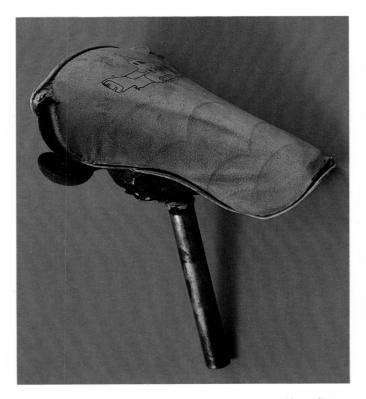

Plate 494. *Bicycle Seat.* Good, $500.00; Excellent/Mint, $650.00.

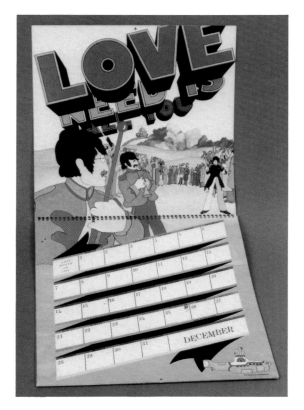

Plate 496. *Candle* is encased in a glass cylinder. This item is one of the rarest Yellow Submarine items. Good, $700.00; Excellent/Mint, $750.00.

Plate 495. *Calendar* was produced by Golden Press. It is spiral-bound. Each month displays a different movie scene. Good, $235.00; Excellent/Mint, $265.00

Plate 497. *Cereal Boxes* graphics were on the back of Wheat and Rice Honeys and were used to advertise rub-ons. Good, $2,000.00; Excellent/Mint, $3,000.00.

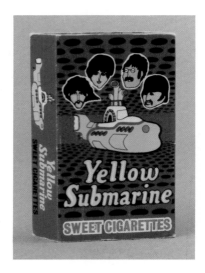

Plate 498. *Cigarettes* were made by Primrose Confectionary. The box contained 10 candy cigarettes. Good, $150.00; Excellent/Mint, $175.00.

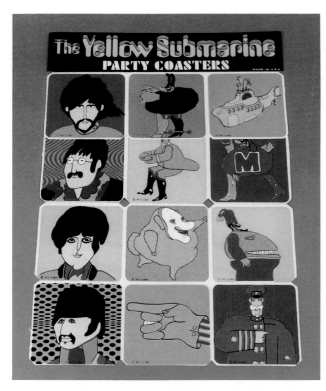

Plate 499. *Coasters* were made by K. Cennar and were manufactured in twelve different subjects. Good, $100.00; Excellent/Mint, $115.00.

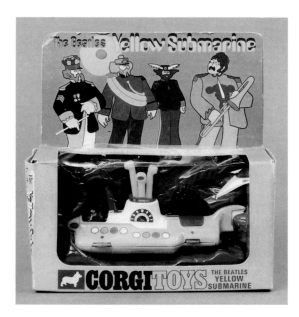

Plate 500. *Corgi Yellow Sub* that came in its original graphic box. Corgi reproduced this sub in the summer of 1997. Good, $800.00; Excellent/Mint, $850.00.

Plate 501. *Comic* was made by Dell and included a poster. Good, $200.00; Excellent/Mint, $400.00.

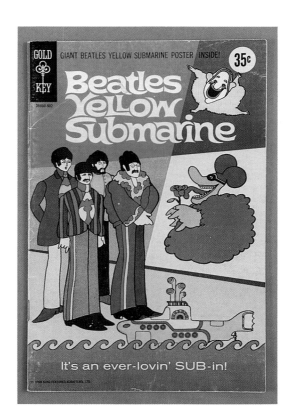

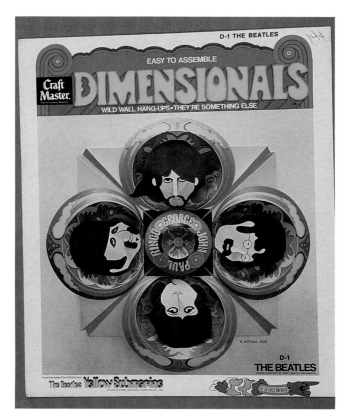

Plate 502. *Dimensionals* were made by Craft Master Paper. When constructed, it makes a colorful wall hanging. Good, $500.00; Excellent/Mint, $550.00.

Plate 503. *Dimensionals* were made by Craft Master Paper. When constructed, it makes a colorful wall hanging. Good, $500.00; Excellent/Mint, $550.00.

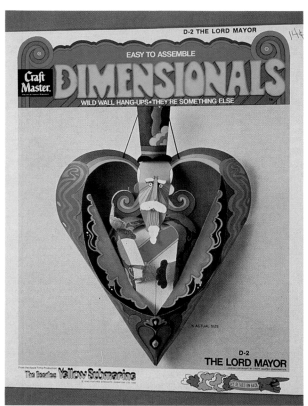

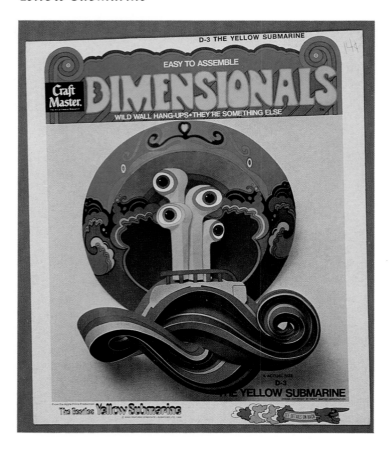

Plate 504. *Dimensionals* were made by Craft Master Paper. When constructed, it makes a colorful wall hanging. Good, $500.00; Excellent/Mint, $550.00.

Plate 505. *Dimensionals* were made by Craft Master Paper. When constructed, it makes a colorful wall hanging. Good, $500.00; Excellent/Mint, $550.00.

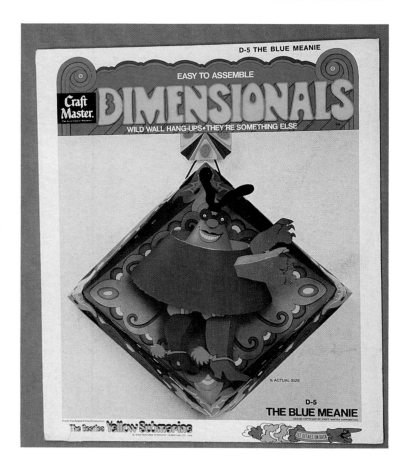

Plate 506. *Dimensionals* were made by Craft Master Paper. When constructed, it makes a colorful wall hanging. Good, $500.00; Excellent/Mint, $550.00.

Plate 507. *Dimensionals* were made by Craft Master Paper. When constructed, it makes a colorful wall hanging. Good, $500.00; Excellent/Mint, $550.00.

Plate 508. *Desk Set Items* are almost impossible to find. (A) Letter Holder, Good, $700.00; Excellent/Mint, $750.00. (B) Tin Pencil Holder, Good, $1,200.00; Excellent/Mint, $1,500.00. (C) Note Pad, Good, $700.00; Excellent/Mint, $750.00.

Plate 509. *Greeting Cards* came in a variety of boxes. Good, $130.00; Excellent/Mint, $140.00.

Plate 510. *Greeting Cards* were made by Sunshine Card Company. Good, $130.00; Excellent/Mint, $140.00.

Plate 511. *Greeting Cards* were made by Sunshine Card Company. Good, $130.00; Excellent/Mint, $140.00.

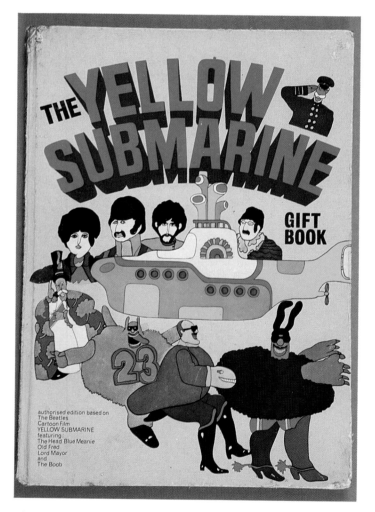

Plate 512. *Yellow Sub Gift Book.* Good, $200.00; Excellent/Mint, $225.00.

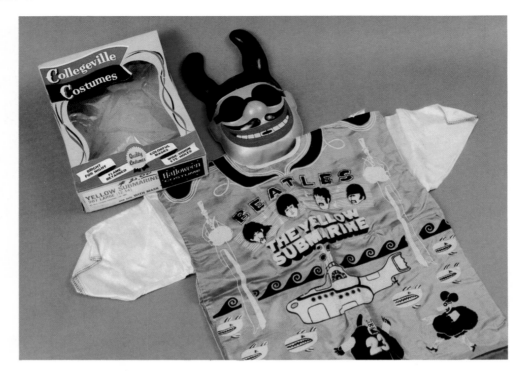

Plate 513. *Halloween Costume* was made by Collegeville Costumes. The Blue Meanie was the only character costume produced. Good, $850.00; Excellent/Mint, $950.00.

Plate 514. *Halloween Costume* was made by Collegeville Costumes. Good, $850.00; Excellent/Mint, $900.00.

Plate 516. *Hanger* (John). Good, $200.00; Excellent/Mint, $225.00.

Plate 515. *Hanger* (Paul) was made by Henderson-Haggard, Inc. The hanger is 16" tall. Good, $200.00; Excellent/Mint, $225.00..

Plate 518. *Hanger* (Ringo) has the image on both sides. Good, $200.00; Excellent/Mint, $225.00.

Plate 517. *Hanger* (George). Good, $200.00; Excellent/Mint, $225.00.

Plate 519. *Keychains* were made by Pride Creations. Good, $8.00; Excellent/Mint, $10.00.

Plate 520. *Keychains* were made by Pride Creations. Good, $20.00; Excellent/Mint, $25.00.

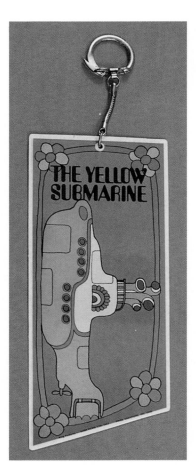

Plate 521. *Yellow Sub Key Chain.* Good, $50.00; Excellent/Mint, $75.00.

Plate 522. *Lobby Cards* were used with the release of "Yellow Submarine." These are the rarer British version. Good, $300.00; Excellent/Mint, $350.00 Each.

Plate 523. *Lobby Cards* were used with the release of "Yellow Submarine." These are the rarer British version. Good, $300.00; Excellent/Mint, $350.00 each.

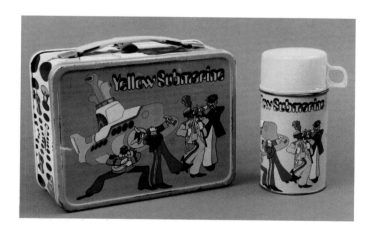

Plate 524. *Lunchbox* was made by King Seeley. The thermos pictured accompanied the lunch box. Good, $750.00; Excellent/Mint, $800.00.

Plate 525. *Mobile* was made by Sunshine Art Studios. When assembled, figures are connected by a black string. Good, $220.00; Excellent/Mint, $230.00.

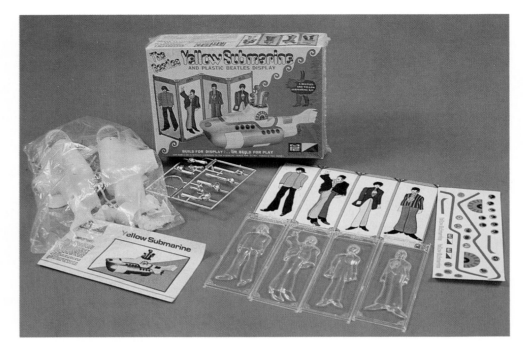

Plate 526. *Model* was made by Model Products Corporation. It came with plastic Beatles. Good, $260.00; Excellent/Mint, $275.00.

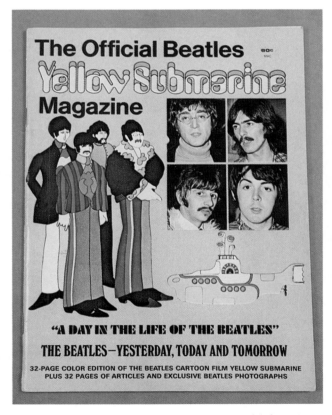

Plate 527. *Yellow Submarine Magazine* sold for 80¢ in 1968. Good, $300.00; Excellent/Mint, $325.00.

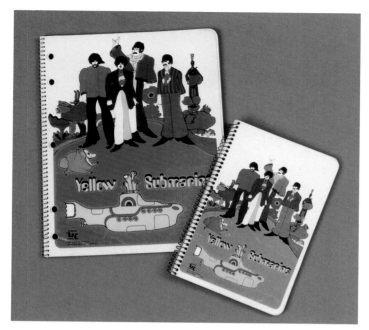

Plate 528. *Notebooks* were made by Vernon Royal and show the two spiral-bound sizes produced. Good, $175.00; Excellent/Mint, $200.00.

Plate 529. *Pencil Holder* is one of the harder to find Yellow Sub items. Good, $600.00; Excellent/Mint, $625.00.

Plate 530. *Photo Album* is the smaller version that could hold 12 photos and came with a small plastic case. Good, $500.00; Excellent/Mint, $525.00.

Plate 531. *Photo Album* is the larger size. Good, $600.00; Excellent/Mint, $675.00.

Plate 532. *Pop-out*s are art decorations. Good, $30.00; Excellent/Mint, $35.00.

Plate 533. *Put-Ons* were made by Craft Master. There were 60 stickers that attached to the poster included. Good, $400.00; Excellent/Mint, $425.00.

Plate 534. *Put-Ons* were made by Craft Master. There were 60 stickers that attached to the poster included. Good, $400.00; Excellent/Mint, $425.00.

Plate 535. *Postcards*. Good, $60.00. Excellent/Mint, $65.00.

Plate 536. *Postcards*. Good, $60.00. Excellent/Mint, $65.00.

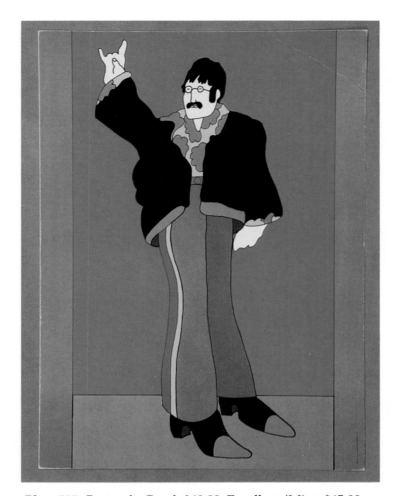

Plate 537. *Postcards.* Good, $60.00. Excellent/Mint, $65.00.

Plate 538. *Postcards.* Good, $60.00. Excellent/Mint, $65.00.

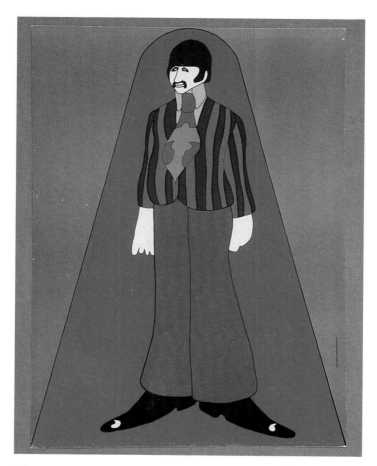

Plate 539. *Postcards.* Good, $60.00. Excellent/Mint, $65.00.

Plate 540. *Puzzle* (In the Yellow Sub) has 650 pieces and measures 19" x 19". Good, $125.00; Excellent/Mint, $150.00.

Plate 541. *Puzzle* (Sgt. Pepper Band) has 160 pieces and was made by Jaymar. Good, $100.00; Excellent/Mint, $125.00.

Plate 542. *Puzzle* (Sea of Monsters) has over 650 pieces and is 19" x 19". Good, $125.00; Excellent/Mint, $150.00.

Plate 543. *Puzzle* (Beatles in Pepperland). Good, $100.00; Excellent/Mint, $125.00.

Plate 544. *Puzzle* (Sea of Monsters). Good, $100.00; Excellent/Mint, $125.00.

Plate 546. *Puzzle* (Blue Meanies Attack). Good, $125.00; Excellent/Mint, $150.00.

Plate 545. *Puzzle* (Meanies Invade Pepperland). Good, $125.00; Excellent/Mint, $150.00.

Plate 547. *Puzzle* (Beatles in Pepperland) is an example of the Bantam Pocket Puzzle. Good, $115.00; Excellent/Mint, $125.00.

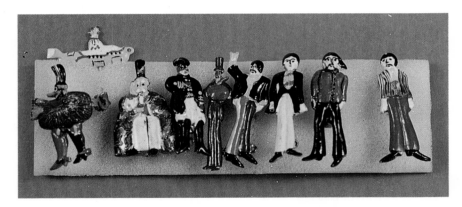

Plate 548. *Yellow Sub Pin Set.* Good, $75.00; Excellent/Mint, $100.00.

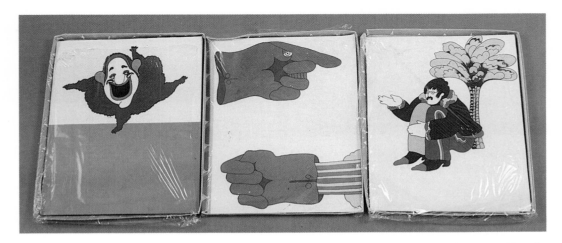

Plate 549. *Stationery* was manufactured by Unicorn Creations. Good, $135.00. Excellent/Mint, $150.00.

Plate 550. *Stationery* was manufactured by Unicorn Creations. Good, $135.00. Excellent/Mint, $150.00.

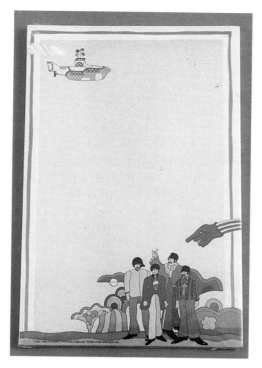

Plate 551. *Stationery* was manufactured by Unicorn Creations. Good, $135.00. Excellent/Mint, $150.00.

Plate 552. *Stationery* was manufactured by Unicorn Creations. Good, $135.00. Excellent/Mint, $150.00.

Plate 553. *Stationery* was manufactured by Unicorn Creations. Good, $135.00. Excellent/Mint, $150.00.

Plate 554. *Stick-ons* were made by Dal Manufacturing Corporation and came with instruction sheet suggesting good
places to stick them. Good, $75.00; Excellent/Mint, $80.00.

Plate 555. *Stick-ons.* Good, $75.00;
Excellent/Mint, $80.00.

Plate 556. *Switch Plate Covers* were made by
Dal Manufacturing Corporation. They are
heavy cardboard. Good, $125.00; Excel-
lent/Mint, $150.00 each.

Plate 557. *Tie Tac Pin* was licensed by King Features Syndicate. Good, $70.00; Excellent/Mint, $80.00.

Plate 558. *Wall Plaque* (Yellow Sub). Good, $125.00; Excellent/Mint, $150.00.

Plate 560. *Watercolor Set* was made by Craft Master. Good, $145.00; Excellent/Mint, $155.00.

Plate 559. *Water Color Set* was made by Craft Master. Good, $135.00; Excellent/Mint, $145.00.

Plate 561. *Scrapbook* is made of hard cardboard. Good, $650.00; Excellent/Mint, $750.00.

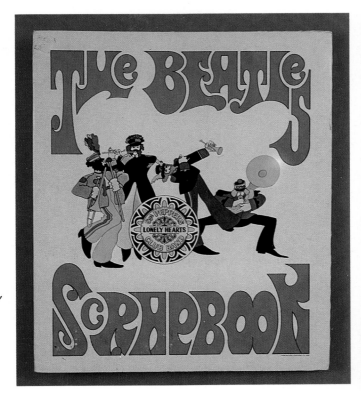

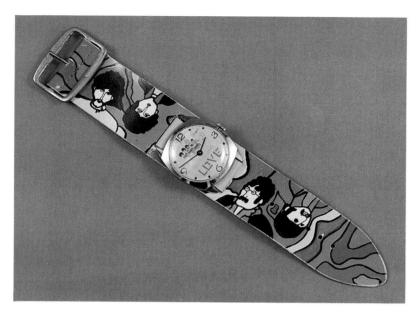

Plate 562. *Yellow Sub Watch* is impossible to find in good condition with its original band. Good, $1,300.00; Excellent/Mint, $1,500.00.

Plate 563. *Yellow Sub Campaign Book.* Good, $400.00; Excellent/Mint, $425.00.

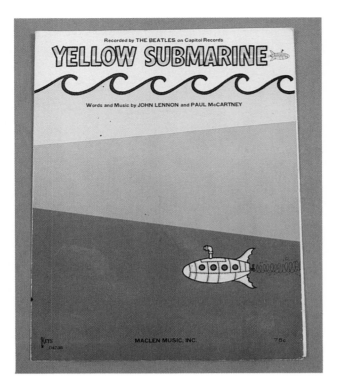

Plate 564. *Yellow Submarine Sheet Music.* Good, $50.00; Excellent/Mint, $75.00.

Plate 565. *Yellow Submarine Model* used in the Los Angeles premiere of movie. This measures 8½' long by 3½' tall. It is made of paper mâché and is a one-of-a-kind item. $25,000.00.

Plate 567. *Blue Meanie Hand Puppet.* Good, $350.00; Excellent/Mint, $400.00.

Plate 566. *Yellow Submarine Model* used in the Los Angeles premiere of movie. This measures 8½' long by 3½' tall. It is made of paper mâché and is a one-of-a-kind item. $25,000.00.

Plate 568. *Yellow Submarine Glove Puppet Box* by Bellamy. This is the only box known to exist and contains Jellybeans and other assorted candy. Good, $2,000.00; Excellent/Mint, $2,500.00.

CHAPTER FIVE

Apple Studio

Promotional items produced by Apple Studios are very collectible. Many were produced in limited numbers and some were given as gifts making them exceedingly rare.

Most Apple items were used as promotional pieces and were not designed for retail sale. An Apple memento value is based more along the pricing of a personal Beatle piece.

Plate 569. *Brass Apple* was given out at the opening of Apple Studios. It is believed that there were one hundred of these produced. Good. $2,000.00; Excellent/Mint, $2,200.00.

Plate 570. *Cube* was sent by Apple Records as part of a fan club promotion. Good, $40.00; Excellent/Mint, $45.00.

Plate 571. *Merry Christmas Apple* is made of foam rubber and was given out as a Christmas gift by the studio. Good, $1,800.00; Excellent/Mint, $2,000.00.

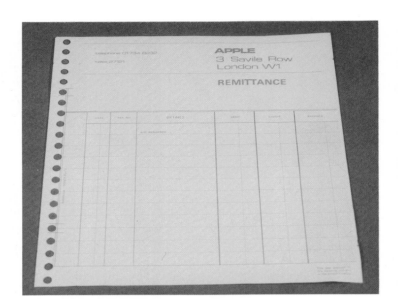

Plate 572. *Remittance* is an actual form used by Apple Studio to record their artists' expenses. Good, $60.00; Excellent/Mint, $65.00.

Plate 573. *Stickers* used by Apple with theme "Stick a garden on something you love." Good, $70.00; Excellent/Mint, $75.00.

Plate 574. *Apple Paperweight* is lucite and was given out by Apple executives. Good, $600.00; Excellent/Mint, $650.00.

Plate 575. *Apple Shirt* was sold in the Apple Boutique in London. Good, $250.00; Excellent/Mint, $275.00.

Plate 576. *Apple Jacket* was sold in the Apple Boutique in London. Good, $350.00; Excellent/Mint, $375.00.

Plate 578. *Apple Record Holders.* Good, $35.00; Excellent/Mint, $40.00.

Plate 577. *Apple Radio* is one of the rarest Apple promotional items. Good, $1,500.00; Excellent/Mint, $1,700.00.

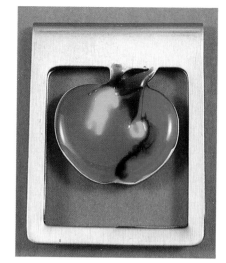

Plate 579. *Apple Money Clip.* Good, $300.00;
Excellent/Mint, $350.00.

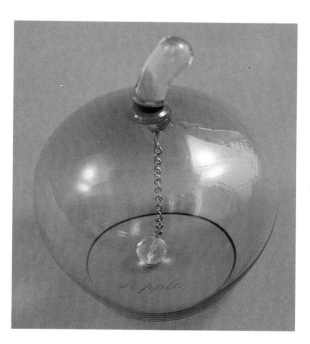

Plate 580. *Glass Apple* was made by Steuben and given out
by the Beatles to a very select group of people. Good,
$3,000.00; Excellent/Mint, $3,500.00.

Plate 581. *Apple Playing Cards.* Good, $125.00;
Excellent/Mint, $150.00.

Plate 582. *Apple Matches* were given out as a holiday gift. Good, $150.00; Excellent/Mint, $175.00.

Plate 583. *Apple Underwear* proves that a viable image can be put on anything. Good, $200.00; Excellent/Mint, $225.00.

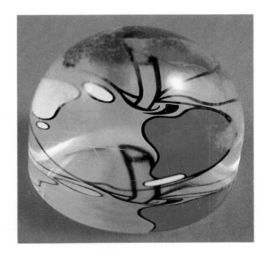

Plate 584. *Apple Paperweight* also came in a green apple variety. Good, $700.00; Excellent/Mint, $750.00.

Plate 585. *Apple Mirror* comes with a stand. Good, $600.00; Excellent/Mint, $700.00.

Plate 586. *Apple Record Crate* was used to send albums to record stores. Good, $175.00; Excellent/Mint, $200.00.

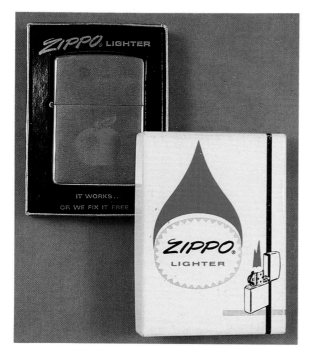

Plate 587. *Apple Lighter* was manufactured by Zippo. Good, $300.00; Excellent/Mint, $350.00.

Plate 588. *Apple Key Chains.* Good, $175.00; Excellent/Mint, $240.00.

CHAPTER SIX

Yellow Submarine Celluloids

Celluloids from the movie "Yellow Submarine" are fast becoming the most popular items of memorabilia. The prices of the cels are increasing at a rapid rate. In the field of Disneyana, cels have always brought the highest prices at auctions.

A cel is a painting on celluloid by studio artists of an animated character or object. It is based on the artist's original pencil drawing. Cels in many cases are shown with backgrounds which were photographed during the productions of the final released versions of a film.

The only original celluloids from the Beatles era are from the only animation feature — "Yellow Submarine." Cels featuring one or more Beatles command much higher prices. A cel showing the yellow submarine is the rarest and most difficult to find.

Plate 589. *Paul Picture.* Good, $1,400.00; Excellent/Mint, $1,700.00.

Plate 590. *(A) Ringo with creature.* Good, $1,000.00; Excellent/Mint, $1,200.00. *(B) Four Beatles.* Good, $1,800.00; Excellent/Mint, $2,000.00.

Plate 592. *Beatle with Apples.* Good, $500.00; Excellent/Mint, $600.00.

Plate 591. ~~Captain Old Fred.~~ ~~Good, $400.00; Excel-~~
~~lent/Mint, $450.00.~~

Plate 594. *Ringo Head Shot.* Good, $400.00; Excellent/Mint, $450.00.

Plate 593. *Ringo.* Good, $1,000.00; Excellent/Mint, $1,100.00.

Plate 595. *Ringo with Original Background.* Good, $2,500.00; Excellent/Mint, $2,800.00.

Plate 596. *Jeremy the Boob.* Good, $350.00; Excellent/Mint, $375.00.

Plate 597. *Dancing Man.* Good, $250.00; Excellent/Mint, $300.00.

Plate 598. *Scene of Two Women.* Good, $400.00; Excellent/Mint, $450.00.

Plate 599. *Flower Man.* Good, $350.00;
Excellent/Mint, $400.00.

Plate 600. *Ringo and John with Hands.* Good, $750.00;
Excellent/Mint, $800.00.

Plate 601. *Beatles with Yellow Sub.* Good,
$2,200.00; Excellent/Mint, $2,500.00.

CHAPTER SEVEN

One of a Kind Items

This chapter deals with items that are considered one-of-a-kind. There are collectors who want only items owned and used by the Beatles. These include automobiles, musical instruments, and clothing. Another field is Beatle autographs, and prices vary greatly on the particular item or piece of paper the autographs were written on.

Gold records given to the Beatles or one of their organizations or record companies are also items that collectors pursue. Beware of forgeries and reproductions. Make sure you receive documentation that your item is genuine.

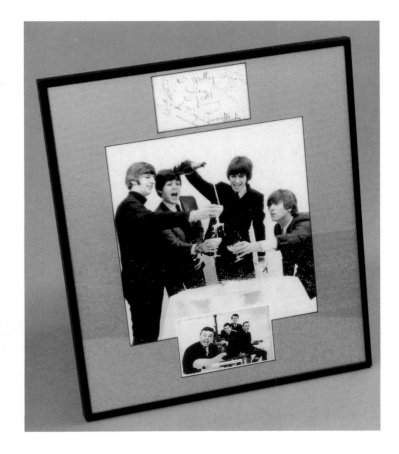

Plate 602. *Beatles Autographs* and Gerry and the Pacemakers autographs. Good, $2,000.00; Excellent/Mint, $2,300.00.

Plate 603. *Beatles Autographs.* Good, $2,500.00; Excellent/Mint, $2,600.00.

Plate 604. *Beatles Autographs.* Good, $2,000.00; Excellent/Mint, $2,200.00.

Plate 605. *Yellow Submarine Gold Record* presented to John Lennon. This is exceedingly rare because it was presented to an actual Beatle. Note the white mat which is indicative of its value. Good, $13,000.00; Excellent/Mint, $15,000.00.

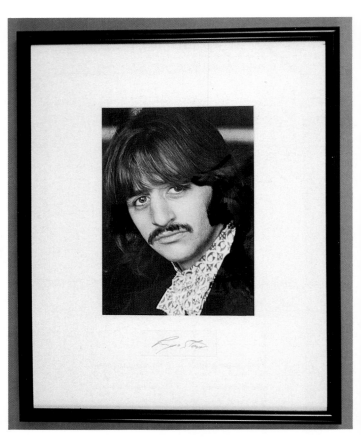

Plate 606. *John Lennon Autograph.* Good, $500.00; Excellent/Mint, $550.00.

Plate 607. *Ringo Starr Autograph.* Good, $400.00; Excellent/Mint, $450.00.

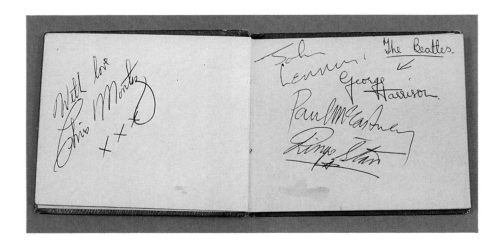

Plate 608. *Beatle Autographs.* Good, $2,500.00; Excellent/Mint, $3,000.00.

Plate 609. *Cavern Brick.* Good, $500.00; Excellent/Mint, $550.00.

Plate 610. *Beat Time Pinball Machine.* Good, $1,500.00; Excellent/Mint, $2,000.00.

Plate 611. *John Lennon Suit*. Good, $10,000.00; Excellent/Mint, $11,000.00.

Plate 612. *Paul McCartney Jacket*. Good, $3,000.00; Excellent/Mint, $3,500.00.

COLLECTOR RESOURCES

The following are reputable dealers that specialize in Beatles memorabilia; the last three have regular phone bid auctions.

BOJO
P.O. Box 1203
Cranberry Turnpike, PA 16033-2203

TIQUES
Highway 34 RRI Box 49B
Oldbridge, NJ 08837
(908) 721-0221

New England Auction Gallery
P.O. Box 2273
W. Peabody, MA 01960-7273

Hake's Americana Collectibles
P.O. Box 1444
York, PA 17405

The authors wish to thank Collector Books for making a dream become a reality. We are already working on Volume Three and desire to purchase any items not found in this volume. Please call or write:

Michael Stern
1950 North Park Place, Suite 100
Atlanta, GA 30339
(770) 951-8411

Author Profiles

Barbara Crawford

Barbara Crawford did all the excellent photography in the book. She is also the proud owner of all the items pictured in this book. Barbara lives in Atlanta, Georgia, with her four dogs and four cats. Barbara has always been an avid Beatle fan. She has almost every piece of recorded music they have done.

Hollis Lamon is a partner with Michael Stern in Lamon & Stern. He is a financial advisor. He is also one of the leading collectors of Yoda memorabilia in the world. Hollis lives in Atlanta with his wife, Jane, and their two sons, Hunter and Austin.

Michael Stern is author of four price guides on Disney toys; Stern's Guide to Disney Collectibles, First, Second, and Third Series, and the Collector's Encyclopedia of Disneyana. He is a financial advisor with Lamon & Stern. Michael resides in Atlanta, with his wife Merrill and twin daughters, Jenny and Lisa. If you have Beatles items to sell or trade, contact him at 1950 North Park Place, Suite 100, Atlanta, GA 30339.

Hollis Lamon

Michael Stern